CW00796253

Apex Design Patterns

Harness the power of Apex design patterns to build robust and scalable code architectures on the Force.com platform

Jitendra Zaa

Anshul Verma

BIRMINGHAM - MUMBAI

Apex Design Patterns

Copyright © 2016 Packt Publishing

All rights reserved. No part of this book may be reproduced, stored in a retrieval system, or transmitted in any form or by any means, without the prior written permission of the publisher, except in the case of brief quotations embedded in critical articles or reviews.

Every effort has been made in the preparation of this book to ensure the accuracy of the information presented. However, the information contained in this book is sold without warranty, either express or implied. Neither the authors, nor Packt Publishing, and its dealers and distributors will be held liable for any damages caused or alleged to be caused directly or indirectly by this book.

Packt Publishing has endeavored to provide trademark information about all of the companies and products mentioned in this book by the appropriate use of capitals. However, Packt Publishing cannot guarantee the accuracy of this information.

First published: April 2016

Production reference: 1220416

Published by Packt Publishing Ltd.

Livery Place

35 Livery Street

Birmingham B3 2PB, UK.

ISBN 978-1-78217-365-6

www.packtpub.com

Credits

Authors

Jitendra Zaa

Anshul Verma

Reviewer

John M. Daniel

Commissioning Editor

Julian Ursell

Acquisition Editor

Nadeem Bagban

Content Development Editor

Aishwarya Pandere

Technical Editor

Madhunikita Sunil Chindarkar

Copy Editor

Rashmi Sawant

Project Coordinator

Nidhi Joshi

Proofreader

Safis Editing

Indexer

Priya Sane

Production Coordinator

Shantanu N. Zagade

Cover Work

Shantanu N. Zagade

About the Authors

Anshul Verma has been working on the Salesforce platform since 2006. Prior to that, he has done extensive development using MS technologies on web, desktop, and mobile applications. He possesses a tremendous understanding of enterprise-scale systems and has worked in designing intricate systems with high scalability, performance, and robustness. He has been a Dreamforce speaker and is a regular contributor to Stack Exchange and other developer communities. He has four Salesforce certifications and is currently working as a project manager and technical architect where he is responsible for managing customer success and delivering high-quality solutions to his clients. He has conducted various training sessions in his current organization and trained over 50 new hires. He is very popular with his training batches and can be often found sharing his knowledge with his team and peers. He owns and maintains his blog (`http://mightycoder.blogspot.com/`), and you can follow him on Twitter at `@toanshulverma`.

Jitendra Zaa has been working on the Salesforce platform since 2008. He has extensively worked on Java and .NET-based enterprise applications. He also has experience in working with multiple JavaScript libraries, web frameworks, ETL tools, and databases. He is an expert in designing and implementing integrations of Salesforce with external systems. He is a regular speaker at the world's biggest developer event, Dreamforce, mostly in developer track. Because of his contributions to the Salesforce community, he has also been awarded the Salesforce MVP title. He has more than eight Salesforce certifications and works as a Salesforce technical architect. He owns one of the most viewed Salesforce developer blogs (`http://www.JitendraZaa.com`), formerly, `http://Shivasoft.in`. You can follow him on Twitter at `@JitendraZaa`.

About the Reviewer

John M. Daniel has been working in the technology sector for over 20+ years. During that time, he has worked with a variety of technologies and project roles. Currently, he works at FinancialForce.com with their Consulting/Product Services teams. He currently holds multiple certifications from Salesforce.com, including the Platform Developer I and II certifications and the Advanced Developer certification. He is currently in the process of attaining the Certified Technical Architect certification. He loves to spend time with his family, swim at the beach, and work on various open source projects, such as ApexDocs and ApexUML. He co-leads his local area Salesforce Developers User Group and can be found on Twitter at `@ImJohnMDaniel`.

John has been a technical reviewer for *Force.com Enterprise Architecture*, by Andrew Fawcett and *Learning Apex Programming*, by Matt Kaufman and Michael Wicherski, both by Packt Publishing.

I would like to thank my wife, Allison, for always giving me the freedom to pursue my interests.

www.PacktPub.com

For support files and downloads related to your book, please visit www.PacktPub.com .

eBooks, discount offers, and more

Did you know that Packt offers eBook versions of every book published, with PDF and ePub files available? You can upgrade to the eBook version at www.PacktPub.com and as a print book customer, you are entitled to a discount on the eBook copy. Get in touch with us at customercare@packtpub.com for more details.

At www.PacktPub.com, you can also read a collection of free technical articles, sign up for a range of free newsletters and receive exclusive discounts and offers on Packt books and eBooks.

https://www2.packtpub.com/books/subscription/packtlib

Do you need instant solutions to your IT questions? PacktLib is Packt's online digital book library. Here, you can search, access, and read Packt's entire library of books.

Why subscribe?

- Fully searchable across every book published by Packt
- Copy and paste, print, and bookmark content
- On demand and accessible via a web browser

Free access for Packt account holders

Get notified! Find out when new books are published by following @PacktEnterprise on Twitter or the Packt Enterprise Facebook page.

Table of Contents

Preface

It was spring 2015; we were both discussing our presentation for Dreamforce 2015. During the discussion, we stumbled on the topic of the usage of design patterns in Apex. We observed that design patterns are still not extensively used in the Apex programming arena. We think that a few prominent factors for this situation are that there are not enough resources available around the design pattern implementation in Apex. Secondly, most of the Apex programmers who started their development career with Force.com have less exposure to other development platforms. Thirdly, some of the design patterns simply do not apply to Force.com development platforms.

As per our observation, the usage and mention of design patterns in day-to-day programming is reduced in Apex as compared to other development platforms. Developers coming from other programming backgrounds mostly have a working experience with design patterns and it's implicit for them to use it in their code style and design.

We realized that it would be even better to develop content around the design pattern implementation in a language that Apex developers can easily relate to. We positively think that by providing scenarios that are specific to Apex development use cases, developers will be able to understand and implement the design patterns in Apex with ease.

To ensure that we are able to provide information uniformly to all Apex developers irrespective of their experience level, this book also includes general programming best practices, programming principles, OOP concepts, and the usual pitfalls at appropriate places.

In line with our past experience with design pattern learning and implementation is the problem of memorizing the design patterns and situations where they fit in. However, in this book, we took real-life scenarios to explain a situation where an appropriate design pattern will be applied. One can easily relate the design pattern with an example given in this book to identify when it is the time to use that pattern.

Some open source GitHub repository links, Salesforce official developer blogs, and other tips have been shared throughout the book, which can be very helpful in Force.com project development.

What this book covers

Chapter 1, *An Introduction to Apex Design Pattern*, covers the basics of inheritance, abstract classes, polymorphism, cohesion and coupling, and object-oriented design principles.

Chapter 2, *Creational Patterns*, focuses on different ways to instantiate objects to achieve code reusability, ease of maintenance, and loose coupling.

Chapter 3, *Structural Patterns*, explains the design patterns that can solve many situations and problems, which occur during project development in Apex, that demand a change in functionalities and cause a ripple effect on the rest of the system.

Chapter 4, *Behavioral Patterns*, provides a glimpse of some problems, such as double dispatch and code maintenance issues, and explains how to use appropriate design patterns to fix them.

Chapter 5, *Handling Concurrency in Apex*, discusses the design solution for the race condition in concurrency, which can result in data corruption without anyone noticing it.

Chapter 6, *Anti-patterns and Best Practices*, shows some common pitfalls observed during application development in Apex and suggested solutions.

What you need for this book

We need an Internet-enabled computer that is capable of running modern browsers supported by Salesforce. We can use the *developer console* in a browser to write the Apex code in Salesforce.

Interested readers can also use their favorite IDEs, such as Sublime Text, Eclipse, Welkins, Atom, Aside, Cloud9, or BrainEngine.

You will also need a free Salesforce developer account to try all the code snippets and examples provided in this book.

Who this book is for

This book is intended for all Apex developers who want to learn and enhance their Apex code designing skills by applying various design patterns. It can be considered as a stepping stone for beginners or intermediate-level Apex programmers by filling their arsenal with powerful design patterns.

Conventions

In this book, you will find a number of text styles that distinguish between different kinds of information. Here are some examples of these styles and an explanation of their meaning.

Code words in text, database table names, folder names, filenames, file extensions, pathnames, dummy URLs, user input, and Twitter handles are shown as follows: "The `AdminGoldSupportImpl` and `AdminPlatinumSupportImpl` classes are written in the same way."

A block of code is set as follows:

```
public class Mario {
    public void ability(){
        System.debug('I can Walk');
    }
    public void info(){
        System.debug('I am Mario');
    }
}
```

Any command-line input or output is written as follows:

```
$ mkdir css
$ cd css
```

New terms and **important words** are shown in bold.

Warnings or important notes appear in a box like this.

Tips and tricks appear like this.

For this book we have outlined the shortcuts for the Mac OX platform if you are using the Windows version you can find the relevant shortcuts on the WebStorm help page `https:/ /www.jetbrains.com/webstorm/help/keyboard-shortcuts-by-category.html`.

Reader feedback

Feedback from our readers is always welcome. Let us know what you think about this book—what you liked or disliked. Reader feedback is important for us as it helps us develop titles that you will really get the most out of.

To send us general feedback, simply e-mail `feedback@packtpub.com`, and mention the book's title in the subject of your message.

If there is a topic that you have expertise in and you are interested in either writing or contributing to a book, see our author guide at `www.packtpub.com/authors`.

Customer support

Now that you are the proud owner of a Packt book, we have a number of things to help you to get the most from your purchase.

Downloading the example code

You can download the example code files for this book from your account at `http://www. packtpub.com`. If you purchased this book elsewhere, you can visit `http://www.packtpu b.com/support` and register to have the files e-mailed directly to you.

You can download the code files by following these steps:

1. Log in or register to our website using your e-mail address and password.
2. Hover the mouse pointer on the **SUPPORT** tab at the top.
3. Click on **Code Downloads & Errata**.
4. Enter the name of the book in the **Search** box.
5. Select the book for which you're looking to download the code files.
6. Choose from the drop-down menu where you purchased this book from.
7. Click on **Code Download**.

You can also download the code files by clicking on the **Code Files** button on the book's webpage at the Packt Publishing website. This page can be accessed by entering the book's name in the **Search** box. Please note that you need to be logged in to your Packt account.

Once the file is downloaded, please make sure that you unzip or extract the folder using the latest version of:

- WinRAR / 7-Zip for Windows
- Zipeg / iZip / UnRarX for Mac
- 7-Zip / PeaZip for Linux

Downloading the color images of this book

We also provide you with a PDF file that has color images of the screenshots/diagrams used in this book. The color images will help you better understand the changes in the output. You can download this file from `https://www.packtpub.com/sites/default/files/downloads/ApexDesignPatterns_ColorImages.pdf`.

Errata

Although we have taken every care to ensure the accuracy of our content, mistakes do happen. If you find a mistake in one of our books—maybe a mistake in the text or the code—we would be grateful if you could report this to us. By doing so, you can save other readers from frustration and help us improve subsequent versions of this book. If you find any errata, please report them by visiting `http://www.packtpub.com/submit-errata`, selecting your book, clicking on the **Errata Submission Form** link, and entering the details of your errata. Once your errata are verified, your submission will be accepted and the errata will be uploaded to our website or added to any list of existing errata under the Errata section of that title.

To view the previously submitted errata, go to `https://www.packtpub.com/books/content/support` and enter the name of the book in the search field. The required information will appear under the **Errata** section.

Piracy

Piracy of copyrighted material on the Internet is an ongoing problem across all media. At Packt, we take the protection of our copyright and licenses very seriously. If you come across any illegal copies of our works in any form on the Internet, please provide us with the location address or website name immediately so that we can pursue a remedy.

Please contact us at `copyright@packtpub.com` with a link to the suspected pirated material.

We appreciate your help in protecting our authors and our ability to bring you valuable content.

Questions

If you have a problem with any aspect of this book, you can contact us at `questions@packtpub.com`, and we will do our best to address the problem.

1
An Introduction to Apex Design Pattern

We assume that you are reading this book because you have encountered situations where you have had the same design requirement multiple times, or seen a repetitive problem that has always been solved with the same solution. Those design solutions that are applied again and again to the same type of problem are also known as *design patterns*.

To better understand the application of design patterns in everyday life, let's take a look at the example of the ATM machine. Every ATM machine needs to have a slot where an ATM card can be inserted, there is a keypad to enter a secret pin, and there is a panel from where the cash can be dispensed. This core functionality of an ATM machine can be considered as a design pattern. Some banks need extra functionalities, such as bill pay or mobile recharge, and they can simply extend this design pattern as per their requirements.

No one would like to reinvent the wheel if an industry-proven solution already exists for a problem, and using such a proven solution would save them time and effort. Furthermore, it also ensures a scalable, robust, and future-ready solution.

In this book, we will discuss the challenges in application development using Apex, common repetitive problems, and most accepted solutions. We have structured our content considering the Apex development platform and blended it with day-to-day challenges that we face during development.

We will first explain the common concepts of application development, which are the building blocks for design patterns. Understanding these concepts is very important as all the design patterns are combinations of one or more principles explained in a later section.

Innovation

It is not necessary that design patterns should fulfill all requirements so why can't we innovate our own better solution?

Yes, innovation is necessary; and certainly, we can come up with a better design and solution or even a new design pattern. Let's take the preceding example; instead of entering a secret pin, a user can use voice recognition for authentication purposes'. It may look cool to some people, but for many it may be a security concern. Speech recognition may not work because of different accents and so on. My point here is that innovation comes at a cost. In software industry, we don't always have the privilege of time because of project timelines and other dependencies.

Design patterns are age-tested and recommended techniques to address a given problem. They not only help in solving the problem at hand, but also address various possible offshoots of the central problem. Design patterns have also evolved as per requirements and will continue to do so.

Design patterns and learning

We are not suggesting that you have to use only design patterns. Every problem is unique and a design pattern can solve only some part of the problem. However, you need to think, design, and come up with your own version of an extended design. Design patterns are very generic and basic; they mostly guide you through the flow of the creation of an object or manipulate the behavior at runtime or structure your code. A design pattern is not a finished code solution, but it is a recommended code structure. Choosing the right design pattern for a given problem is very important and needs thorough understanding. With increasing use of design patterns, you can further enhance your development skills and understand how to best structure your code.

Object-Oriented Programming (OOP)

Any language that supports the following four pillars of Object-Oriented Programming is known as an **Object-Oriented Programming (OOP)** language:

- **Inheritance**: This is the ability to extend an existing class to add a new functionality
- **Polymorphism**: This is the ability to perform different actions by calling the same method
- **Abstraction**: This is the ability to hide complex implementation
- **Encapsulation**: This is the ability to bind data attributes and behavior together

OOPs in play

Let's take an example of the childhood game *Mario* to understand OOPs. The following class shows some basic information about *Mario* and its capabilities:

```
public class Mario {
    public void ability(){
        System.debug('I can Walk');
    }
    public void info(){
        System.debug('I am Mario');
    }
}
```

This ability to bind the capabilities of *Mario* in the same place is called *encapsulation*.

Like any other games, there are power boosters, such as speed running, bullets, and so on. If we want to change the behavior of *Mario* in the game, some more code can be added to the existing class with conditions. However, the chances are high that an existing application will break due to the introduction of the new code. OOP suggests that you do not modify the existing code but extend it so that testing can be done only on the new code and there are fewer maintenance issues. To resolve this, we can use *Inheritance*.

 To use inheritance in Apex, we need to use the `virtual` or `abstract` keywords in the base class and methods.

To use inheritance, we need to use the `virtual` keyword in the base class and methods. The `virtual` keyword states that a class or method can be inherited and overridden by child classes. We need to make some modification in the preceding `Mario` class, informing Apex about what can be overridden. We only need to override the `ability` method in the child class, so we need to mark it as the `virtual` method. In order to inherit this class, it should also be declared with the `virtual` keyword:

```
public virtual class Mario {
    public virtual void ability(){
        System.debug('I can Walk');
    }
    public void info(){
        System.debug('I am Mario');
    }
}
```

Let's see how a child class can be written in Apex:

```
public class Mario_Run extends Mario {
    public override void ability(){
        super.ability();
        System.debug('I can Run);
    }
}
```

The following figure shows a parent-child relationship between classes:

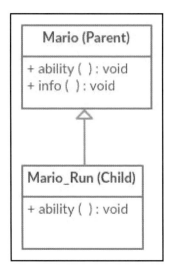

The `extends` keyword is used in a child class to inform a parent class. If we are writing the same method again in a child class of a parent class, then the `override` keyword needs to be used. The `override` keyword informs Apex that this is a new version of the same method in the parent class. If we want to call any method in a parent class, we need to use the `super` keyword.

Run the following code as an anonymous Apex script from the developer console to understand inheritance:

```
Mario obj = new Mario();
obj.info();
obj.ability();
System.debug('----- Mario with power booster ----- ');
obj = new Mario_Run();
obj.info();
obj.ability();
```

The output will look something like this:

```
I am Mario
I can Walk
----- Mario with power booster -----
I am Mario
I can Walk
I can Run
```

As we can see, in the preceding code snippet, a child class is able to reuse a parent class method with an added behavior. The type of object is `Mario`, which is the parent class, but Apex is able to call a method of the `Mario_Run class` using *dynamic dispatch*, which is a kind of *Polymorphism*.

 Assigning a child class reference to a parent class is known as **subtype polymorphism**. Read more about subtype polymorphism at `https://en .wikipedia.org/wiki/Subtyping`.

Static and dynamic dispatch

Types of polymorphism can be identified on the basis of when an *implementation is selected*. In this approach, when an implementation is selected at compile time, it is known as **static dispatch**. When an implementation is selected while a program is running (in case of a virtual method), it is known as **dynamic dispatch**.

An interface

An **interface** is another way to achieve polymorphism and abstraction in Apex. Interfaces are like a contract. We can only add a declaration to a class but not the actual implementation. You might be thinking about why do we need to create a class, which does not have anything in it? Well, I will ask you to think about this again after taking a look at the following example.

We will continue with the *Mario* example. Like any game, this game also needs to have levels. Every level will be different from the previous; and therefore, the code cannot be reused. Inheritance was very powerful because of the *dynamic dispatch* polymorphic behavior; however, inheritance can not be used in this scenario.

We will be using an interface to define levels in a game. Every level will have its number and environment:

```
public interface GameLevel {
    void levelNumber();
    void environment();
}
```

The preceding interface defines two methods that need to be implemented by child classes. The `interface` keyword is used to define an interface in Apex:

```
public class Level_Underground implements GameLevel {
    public void levelNumber(){
        System.debug('Level 1');
    }
    public void environment(){
        System.debug('This level will be played Underground');
    }
}

public class Level_UnderWater implements GameLevel {
    public void levelNumber(){
        System.debug('Level 2');
    }
    public void environment(){
        System.debug('This level will be played Under Water');
    }
}
```

The preceding two classes implement `GameLevel` and make sure that both the methods have been implemented. A compiler will throw an error if there is any mistake in implementing a child class with a different method signature.

The following class diagram shows two classes implementing a common interface:

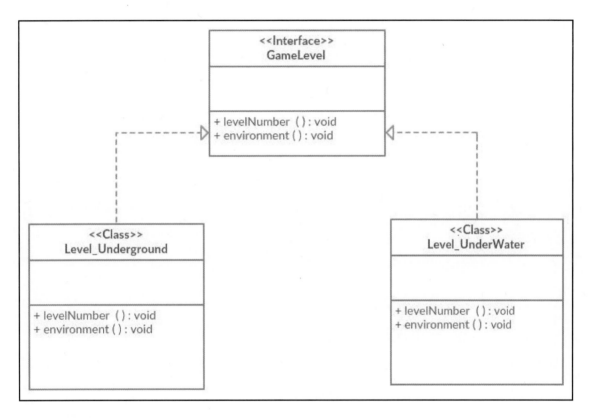

The anonymous Apex code for testing is as follows:

```
GameLevel obj = new Level_Underground();
obj.levelNumber();
obj.environment();
obj = new Level_UnderWater();
obj.levelNumber();
obj.environment();
```

The output of this code snippet is as follows:

```
Level 1
This level will be played Underground
Level 2
This level will be played Under Water
```

We cannot instantiate interfaces; however, we can assign any child class to them; this behavior of an interface makes it a diamond in the sea of OOP.

In the preceding code, `obj` is defined as `GameLevel`; however, we assigned `Level_Underground` and `Level_UnderWater` to it, and Apex was able to dynamically dispatch correct the implementation methods.

Huge applications and APIs are created using interfaces. In Apex, `Queueable` and `Schedulable` are examples of interfaces. Apex only needs to invoke the `execute()` method in your class because it knows that you follow the contract of an interface.

 Apex does not support multiple inheritance where one child class extends multiple parent classes at a time. However, using an interface a child class can implement multiple interfaces at a time.

An abstract class

An abstract class is something between inheritance and an interface. In *inheritance,* a child class extends a parent class, where both the classes have full implementations. In an *interface,* a parent class does not have any implementation and depends on child classes completely. There are scenarios where a parent class knows the common implementations needed by all child classes but the remaining implementation differs for all.

In the same game that we discussed earlier, there are multiple ways to gain points. If *Mario* gets any coin, then the overall score will be added (known), but there are different kinds of coins (unknown). Coins may be in blue, yellow, or different colors. Each color will add different scores.

It's time to see an abstract class in action:

```
public abstract class GameCoin {
  public abstract Integer coinValue();
  public Integer absorbCoin(Integer existingPoint){
    return existingPoint + coinValue();
  }
}
```

The `coinValue` method is declared using the `abstract` keyword, which means that all child classes need to implement this. However, it is known that whatever this method returns, it needs to be added to the existing points; and therefore, the `absorbCoin` method does not need to be written again and again in all child classes. Don't get confused about how we have used an abstract method in `absorbCoin`. Like interfaces, we cannot instantiate an abstract class; therefore, whenever `absorbCoin()` is called from a child class, it will be implemented.

Let's play it out:

```
public class BlueCoin extends GameCoin{
    public override Integer coinValue(){
        return 50;
    }
}

public class YellowCoin extends GameCoin{
    public override Integer coinValue(){
        return 10;
    }
}
```

The preceding two child classes extend the `GameCoin` abstract class.

The anonymous Apex code for testing is as follows:

```
Integer totalPoints = 0;
GameCoin coins = new BlueCoin();
totalPoints = coins.absorbCoin(
  totalPoints);

coins = new YellowCoin();
totalPoints = coins.absorbCoin(totalPoints);

coins = new BlueCoin();
totalPoints = coins.absorbCoin(totalPoints);
System.debug('Total points - ' + totalPoints);
```

The output of this code will be as follows:

```
Total points - 110
```

The following class diagram shows two classes that extend an abstract class and implement an abstract method.

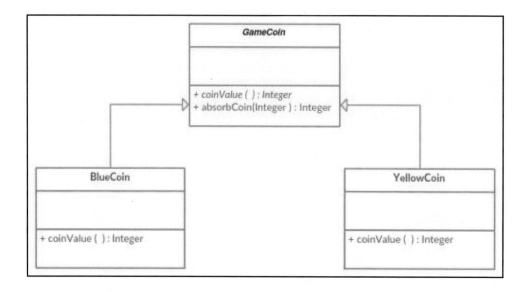

Advantages of design patterns

We all learn programming by making mistakes and learning from all the erroneous code that we develop. There will be situations where you may have faced a particular problem multiple times. Now, we have a clear approach on how to address the issue. A design pattern is designed, implemented, and verified industry wide.

Design patterns not only bring standardization to your code, but also ensure that your code follows good programming principles, such as **coupling** and **cohesion**.

Coupling measures the dependency of software components on each other. So, in essence, this is how two components interact with each other and pass information. High coupling leads to complex code. Practically, components need to communicate with each other, so dependency cannot be entirely removed. It also indicates the robustness of the code, that is, the impact it has on a component if any related component is modified. Hence, low coupling indicates a good code structure. Just imagine that you have a controller that calls a service class, which further calls another controller. So, effectively, the first controller is indirectly dependent on the second controller. With high coupling:

- Code maintenance can be tedious work
- Any change can have a ripple effect on the entire system
- There is less reusability of code

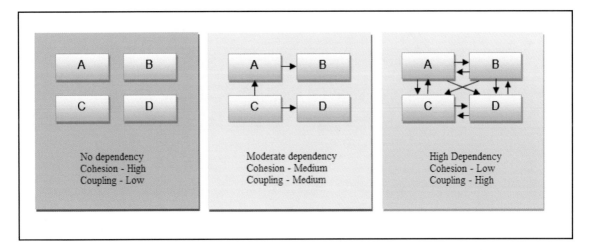

Cohesion measures the degree to which a code component has been well built and focused. As per object-oriented design principle, **encapsulation**, all the related data and functionalities should be encapsulated in the same program component (for example, a class). It ensures that all related functionalities are present in one place and controls their accessibility. This enhances the robustness of the code and imparts modularity to the final product. Lower code cohesion indicates lower dependency of modules/classes, that is, higher maintainability, less complexity, and lesser impact on the part of change.

In short, high cohesion is better for you and indicates that a class is doing a well-defined job. Low cohesion means that a class is doing many jobs with little in common between jobs.

The following code snippet is an example of high cohesion:

```
class AccountService{

  public Account createAccount(){
  // business logic
  }

  public Opportunity createOpportunity(){
  // business logic
  }

  public Contact createContact(){
  // business logic
  }
}
```

In the preceding code snippet, notice that the `AccountService` class tends to be a *jack of all trades*, that is, it tries to solve multiple objectives. This leads to further confusion between method calls and makes maintenance tedious.

The following code snippet is an example of low cohesion:

```
class AccountService{

  public Account createAccount(){
  // business logic
  }
}

class OpportunityService
  public Opportunity createOpportunity(){
  // business logic
  }
}

class ContactService
  public Contact createContact(){
  // business logic
  }
}
```

The following diagram shows how we converted **low cohesion** to **high cohesion**.

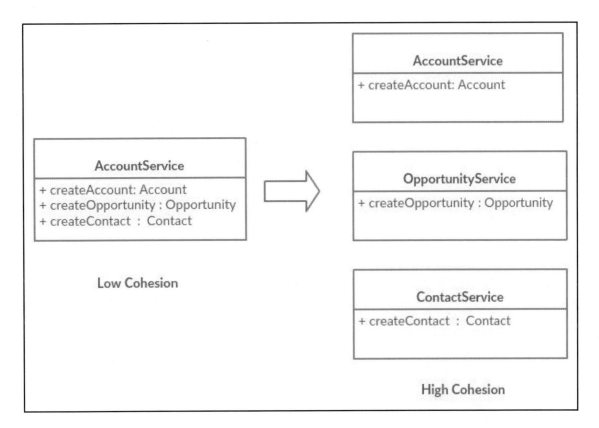

Another advantage of using design patterns is that if testers know that a specific design pattern is used in an implementation, they can quickly relate to it. According to their past experience with design patterns, they can easily identify possible failure scenarios.

Next in the list of advantages is communication and support. Design patterns are well-known in the developer community and forums. Also, they can be easily discussed with your technical lead, project manager, test lead, or architects. When someone new joins your development team, usage of design patterns can help describe the code base to the new team member and aid in a developer's ramp up and acclimation.

Design patterns and Apex

Apex is a proprietary programming language for Salesforce and, therefore, is different from other programming languages, such as Java, C#, and C. Even though the syntax of Apex resembles to Java and C#; however, programming on the Force.com platform is quite different. We will discuss many standard design patterns in the next section of this chapter; however, every pattern may not be suitable for Apex.

A few important differences between Apex and other **Object-Oriented Programming (OOP)** languages are as follows:

- Apex runs on the multi-tenant platform; therefore, in order to make sure that other tenants are not impacted, Salesforce enforces various limits. As developers, we need to make sure that our code does not breach any governor limits.
- Other programming languages do not mandate code coverage for deployments. However, in the case of Salesforce, the Apex code needs to have a minimum code coverage of 75% (the entire code in the environment) for production deployments.
- Static variables in Java persist until the **Java Virtual Machine (JVM)** execution lifespan, which may last from days to months or even years. In the case of Apex, a static variable lasts for the duration of an individual user request execution only (until the time the user request is being processed on a server).

 Governor limits are Salesforce's way to force programmers to write efficient code. As Apex runs in a multitenant environment, a strict enforcement of all limits becomes a necessity for the Apex runtime engine so that no code monopolizes the shared resources. If because of a bad design or nonrecommended architecture, any code does not comply with governor limits, the Apex runtime throws a runtime exception, which cannot be handled within Apex. Apex also exposes many limit methods to check the limit consumption. Read more about this in detail at `https://d eveloper.salesforce.com/docs/atlas.en-us.apexcode.meta/ap excode/apex_gov_limits.htm`.

Gang of Four (GoF)

Design patterns in computer science achieved prominence when *Design Pattern: Elements of Reusable Object-Oriented Software* was published in 1994 by authors Erich Gamma, Richard Helm, Ralph Johnson, and John Vlissides. These authors are also known as the **Gang of Four (GoF)**.

This book contains 23 classic design patterns. After this book, many programmers adopted and created their own design patterns, referring to these classic patterns as bases.

Instead of memorizing exact classes, methods, and properties in design patterns, it is very important to understand the concept and where to apply it appropriately. Incorrect, unsuitable, or unnecessary usage of design patterns can over complicate your code and may result in code that is hard to maintain and debug.

A design pattern is a tool. As with any tool, its performance depends on its usage and the user who is using it.

Gang of Four design patterns are divided into the following three categories:

- The creational pattern
- The structural pattern
- The behavioral pattern

The following figure shows a summary of the design patterns and their categories:

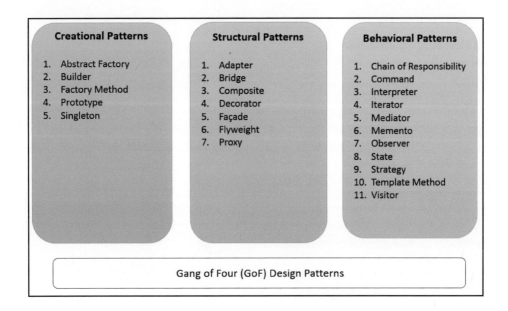

Creational Patterns	Structural Patterns	Behavioral Patterns
1. Abstract Factory	1. Adapter	1. Chain of Responsibility
2. Builder	2. Bridge	2. Command
3. Factory Method	3. Composite	3. Interpreter
4. Prototype	4. Decorator	4. Iterator
5. Singleton	5. Façade	5. Mediator
	6. Flyweight	6. Memento
	7. Proxy	7. Observer
		8. State
		9. Strategy
		10. Template Method
		11. Visitor

Gang of Four (GoF) Design Patterns

The SOLID principle

SOLID is short for basic five principles of OOP, which was introduced in the early 2000s and adopted widely in the software industry. When these principles are combined together, a programmer can create an application that will be easy to maintain and can be extended over time.

The SOLID abbreviation is defined as follows:

- **S**: Single responsibility principle
- **O**: Open closed principle
- **L**: Liskov substitution principle
- **I**: Interface segregation principle
- **D**: Dependency inversion principle

The single responsibility principle (SRP)

This states that *a class should have only one reason to change it, and this means, it should have a single job.*

If we can write code for multiple functionalities in a class, it doesn't mean that we should. Smaller classes and smaller methods will give us more flexibility, and we don't have to write a lot of extra code. It saves us from over complicating classes and helps in achieving high cohesion.

For example, the `Person` class has the code to show the available balance and deduct it from `Account`. This is a clear violation of SRP. This class has two reasons to change: if any attribute of `Person` changes or any information about `Account` changes.

The advantages of SRP are as follows:

- It makes code as easy as possible to reuse
- Small classes can be changed easily
- Small classes are more readable

Splitting classes is a way to implement SRP. Another example of the SRP violation is *God classes*, which we will discuss in the next chapter.

The open closed principle (OCP)

This states that *entities of software, such as classes and methods, should be open for extension but closed for modification.* This means that classes and methods should be allowed to be extended without modification.

For example, a class returns report data in the string and XML formats. In future, we may want to return data in the JSON or CSV format. We should not modify the existing class as it may have an impact on all the other classes using it. It would be a violation of OCP.

The importance of OCP lies in the following scenarios:

- Any changes made in any existing code can potentially impact the entire system
- In some conditions, we cannot change code (the managed package in Apex), so OCP is implied

We can implement OCP using design patterns, such as the *strategy pattern*. In the preceding scenario, we can create an interface of the `ReportData` type and different classes implementing that interface to return different report formats. We will discuss this in more detail in the upcoming chapters.

The Liskov substitution principle (LSP)

This states that *if class B is a child of class A, then A can be replaced by B, without changing anything in a program.* In other words, the LSP principle states that you should not encounter unexpected results if child (derived) classes are used instead of parent classes.

This principle is also known as **Substitutability** and was introduced by **Barbara Liskov** in 1987. This is one of the most widely used principles in programming. You might be already using this, but may not know that it is called LSP.

For example, let's say that we have a `Customer_Ticket` class defined to close a case using the `close()` method. A `Customet_Ticket_Escalated` child class is defined as well to handle an escalated case; however, it cannot close a case by a normal process because the customer was not happy. If we substitute a parent class by this child class and call the `close()` method, it will throw an exception, which is a clear violation of LSP.

The following code snippet explains this scenario:

```
public virual class Customer_Ticket{
    String status ;
    public virtual void close(){
        status = 'close';
```

```
        }
        //other code
    }

    public class Customet_Ticket_Escalated extends Customer_Ticket{
        public override void close(){
            throw new Exception('As this is escalated case therefore
                cannot be closed by normal process');
        }
        //other code
    }
```

The anonymous Apex code for testing is as follows:

```
    Customer_Ticket issue = new Customet_Ticket_Escalated();
    issue.close();//runtime exception, violation of LSP
```

To implement LSP, a proper use of inheritance with a protected access specifier is needed, and a parent class should not have any attributes, which may not apply to every child class.

The interface segregation principle (ISP)

This states that *do not force a child class to depend on a method that is not used for them*. This principle suggests that you break interfaces into smaller ones so that a client can only implement an interface that is of interest. This principle is very similar to the **high cohesive** principle, as discussed earlier.

One way to identify the ISP violation is *if we implement any interface or derive a base class where we need to throw an exception for an unsupported operation*.

The ISP are as follows:

- It enforces the single responsibility principle for interfaces and base classes
- Any changes made in the interface may affect child classes even though they are not using unused methods

For example, `Product` is an interface and contains the `Name` and `Author` attributes. Two child classes named `Movie` and `Book` are derived from `Product`. However, `Movie` is a `Product` but does not have an author, and therefore a runtime exception would be thrown if it's used.

The following example shows the valid and invalid code according to the ISP:

Violation of ISP	Adheres ISP

``
Public interface Product{
   Public String getName();
   Public String getAuthor();
}
 	
Public Class Movie implements Product{
   private String movieName;
   private String author;
 	
   Public String getName(){
      return movieName;
   }
 	
   Public String getAuthor(){
      return new CustomException('Method not Supported');
   }
}
``
	``
	Public interface Product{
	   Public String getName();
	   Public String getAuthor();
	}
	
	Public Class Book implements Product{
	   private String bookName;
	   private String author;
	   Public String getName(){
	      return bookName;
	   }
	
	   Public String getAuthor(){
	      return author;
	   }
	}
	``

Anonymous apex code for testing is as follows:
 	
``
Product m = new Movie();
m.getAuthor();//runtime exception
``
	Anonymous apex code for testing is as follows:
	
	``
	Product p = new Book();
	p.getAuthor(); //works
	``

The dependency inversion principle (DIP)

This states that *modules should not depend on each other directly and should depend via an interface (abstraction).*

In other words, two classes should not be tightly coupled. Tightly coupled classes cannot work independently of each other, and if a change is required, then it creates a wave of changes throughout the application.

One way to identify a DIP violation is the *use of a new keyword in the same class*. If we are using a new keyword, then this means that we are trying to instantiate a class directly. We can create a container class to delegate the creation of a new object. This class will know how to instantiate another class on the basis of the interface type. This approach is also known as **dependency injection** or **Inversion of Control (IoC)**. If you know about the trigger factory pattern that is widely used in Apex, then you may be able to relate with it, else we will discuss this in the upcoming chapters.

For example, in the real world you would not want to solder a lamp directly to the electrical wiring; we would rather use a plug so that the lamp can be used in any electric outlet. In this case, the lamp and electric outlet are the class and the plug is the interface.

Class A should not know any details about how class B is implemented. An interface should be used for communication. As discussed earlier, if needed we can always create a new child class from the interface and use it as per the LSP principle.

The following screenshot shows a scenario before and after DIP. In the first case, the Apex scheduler directly uses classes to calculate sharing and assigns a record to the user. All three classes are tightly coupled in this case. As per DIP, we need to introduce interfaces between them so that classes do not depend on implementation, but they will depend on the abstraction (interface).

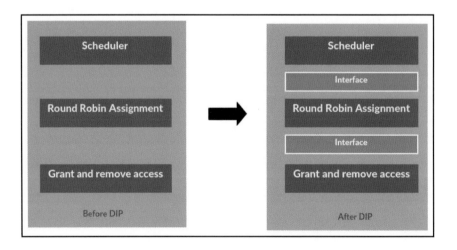

Downloading the example code

You can download the example code files for this book from your account at http://www.packtpub.com. If you purchased this book elsewhere, you can visit http://www.packtpub.com/support and register to have the files e-mailed directly to you.

You can download the code files by following these steps:

1. Log in or register to our website using your e-mail address and password.
2. Hover the mouse pointer on the SUPPORT tab at the top.
3. Click on Code Downloads & Errata.
4. Enter the name of the book in the Search box.
5. Select the book for which you're looking to download the code files.
6. Choose from the drop-down menu where you purchased this book from.
7. Click on Code Download.

You can also download the code files by clicking on the Code Files button on the book's webpage at the Packt Publishing website. This page can be accessed by entering the book's name in the Search box. Please note that you need to be logged in to your Packt account.

Once the file is downloaded, please make sure that you unzip or extract the folder using the latest version of:

- WinRAR / 7-Zip for Windows
- Zipeg / iZip / UnRarX for Mac
- 7-Zip / PeaZip for Linux

The advantages of DIP are as follows:

- Tight coupling is bad and everyone knows this
- It's harder to write test classes as implementation details need to be known for other dependent classes
- If DIP is followed, fake test records can be supplied to classes directly without knowing the implementation details

Summary

In this chapter, we discussed design patterns and why we need their categories and types. In the next chapter, we will discuss the common challenges faced while creating objects and their solutions using design patterns. So, basically, the next chapter will focus completely on creational design patterns.

2
Creational Patterns

Apex programming revolves around objects and classes. During the course of application development, we create multiple classes. Also, we create objects of these classes to satisfy business requirements. Creating an object of a class within another class, creates dependency between those classes. This is also known as **tight coupling**.

As discussed in the previous chapter, tight coupling is considered inferior, as it can negatively impact the code's maintainability and scalability. Creational design patterns can help us avoid tight coupling by hiding the object creational logic.

Creational design patterns can be considered in the following scenarios:

- Instantiating classes in the Apex `Scheduler` class. If we directly instantiate the Apex class in scheduler using new keyword, then the class gets serialized and, therefore, locked for further changes.
- Using multiple classes while creating test data in test classes.
- Creating code libraries only to reveal their usage and not their actual implementation.
- Dynamically creating instances of classes based on the configuration stored in custom settings.

In this chapter, we will discuss some problems that can occur mainly during the creation of class instances and how we can write the code for the creation of objects in a more simple, easy to maintain, and scalable way.

We will discuss the following creational design patterns:

- The factory method pattern
- The abstract factory pattern
- The builder pattern
- The prototype pattern
- The singleton pattern

Factory method pattern

Often, we find that some classes have common features (behavior) and can be considered classes of the same family. For example, multiple payment classes represent a family of payment services. Credit card, debit card, and net banking are some of the examples of payment classes that have common methods, such as `makePayment`, `authorizePayment`, and so on. Using the **factory method pattern**, we can develop controller classes, which can use these payment services, without knowing the actual payment type at design time.

 The factory method pattern is a creational design pattern used to create objects of classes from the same family without knowing the exact class name at design time.

Using the factory method pattern, classes can be instantiated from the common factory method. The advantage of using this pattern is that it delegates the creation of an object to another class and provides a good level of abstraction.

Let's learn this pattern using the following example:

The *Universal Call Center* company is a new business and provides free admin support to customers for resolving issues related to their products. A call center agent can get some information about the available product support; for example, to get the Service Level Agreement (SLA) or information about the total number of open tickets allowed per month.

A developer came up with the following class:

```
public class AdminBasicSupport{
  /**
   *   return SLA in hours
   */
  public Integer getSLA()
  {
    return 40;
```

```
  }
  /**
   * Total allowed support tickets allowed every month
   */
  public Integer allowedTickets(){
    // As this is basic support
    return 9999;
  }
}
```

Now, to get the SLA of `AdminBasicSupport`, we need to use the following code every time:

```
AdminBasicSupport support = new AdminBasicSupport();
System.debug('Support SLA is - '+support.getSLA());

Output - Support SLA is - 40
```

The Universal Call Centre company was doing very well, and in order to grow the business and increase the profit, they started premium support for customers who were willing to pay for cases and get quick support. To make it special and distinct from the basic support, they changed the SLA to 12 hours and a maximum of 50 cases could be opened in one month. A developer had many choices to make this happen in the existing code. However, instead of changing the existing code, they created a new class that would handle only the premium support-related functionalities. This was a good decision because of the single responsibility principle, as discussed in `Chapter 1`, *An Introduction to Apex Design Pattern*:

```
public class AdminPremiumSupport{
  /**
   * return SLA in hours
   */
  public Integer getSLA()
  {
    return 12;
  }
  /**
   * Total allowed support tickets allowed every month is 50
   */
  public Integer allowedTickets()
  {
    return 50;
  }
}
```

Now, every time any information regarding the SLA or allowed tickets per month is needed, the following Apex code can be used:

```
if(Account.supportType__c == 'AdminBasic')
{
  AdminBasicSupport support = new AdminBasicSupport();
  System.debug('Support SLA is - '+support.getSLA());
}else{
  AdminPremiumSupport support = new AdminPremiumSupport();
  System.debug('Support SLA is - '+support.getSLA());
}
```

As we can see in the preceding example, instead of adding some conditions to the existing class, the developer decided to go with a new class. Each class has its own responsibility, and they only need to be changed for one reason. If any change is needed in the basic support, then only one class needs to be changed. As we all know, this design principle is known as the **single responsibility principle**.

Business was doing exceptionally well in the call center, and they planned to start the *gold* and *platinum* support as well. Developers started facing issues with the current approach. Currently, they have two classes for the basic and premium support and requests for two more classes are in the pipeline. There was no guarantee that the support type will not remain the same in future. Because of every new support type, a new class is needed; and therefore, the previous code needs to be updated to instantiate these classes. The following code will be needed to instantiate these classes everywhere:

```
if(Account.supportType__c == 'AdminBasic')
{
  AdminBasicSupport support = new AdminBasicSupport();
  System.debug('Support SLA is - '+support.getSLA());
}else if(Account.supportType__c == 'AdminPremier')
{
  AdminPremiumSupport support = new AdminPremiumSupport();
  System.debug('Support SLA is - '+support.getSLA());
}else if(Account.supportType__c == 'AdminGold')
{
  AdminGoldSupport support = new AdminGoldSupport();
  System.debug('Support SLA is - '+support.getSLA());
}else{
  AdminPlatinumSupport support = new AdminPlatinumSupport();
  System.debug('Support SLA is - '+support.getSLA());
}
```

We are only considering the getSLA() method, but in a real application, there can be other methods and scenarios as well. The preceding code snippet clearly depicts the code duplicity and maintenance nightmare.

The following image shows the overall complexity of the example that we are discussing:

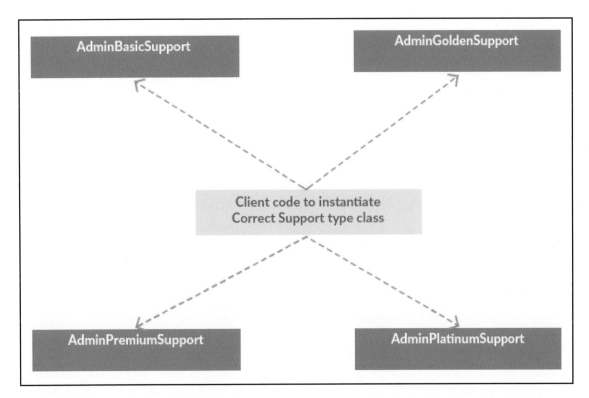

Although they are using a separate class for each support type, an introduction to a new support class will lead to changes in the code in all existing code locations where these classes are being used. The development team started brainstorming to make sure that the code is capable of being extended easily in the future with the least impact on the existing code. One of the developers came up with a suggestion to use an interface for all support classes so that every class can have the same methods and they can be referred to using an interface.

The following interface was finalized to reduce the code duplicity:

```
public Interface IAdminSupport{
   Integer getSLA() ;
   Integer allowedTickets();
}
```

Methods defined within an interface have no access modifiers and just contain their signatures.

Once an interface was created, it was time to update existing classes. In our case, only one line needed to be changed and the remaining part of the code was the same because both the classes already have the `getSLA()` and `allowedTickets()` methods.

Let's take a look at the following line of code:

```
public class AdminPremiumSupport{
```

This will be changed to the following code:

```
public class AdminBasicSupportImpl implements IAdminSupport{
```

The following line of code is as follows:

```
public class AdminPremiumSupport{
```

This will be changed to the following code:

```
public class AdminPremiumSupportImpl implements IAdminSupport{
```

The `AdminGoldSupportImpl` and `AdminPlatinumSupportImpl` classes are written in the same way.

 A class diagram is a type of **Unified Modeling Language** (**UML**), which describes classes, methods, attributes, and their relationships among other objects in a system. You can read more about class diagrams at `https://e n.wikipedia.org/wiki/Class_diagram`.

The following image shows a class diagram of the code written by developers using an interface:

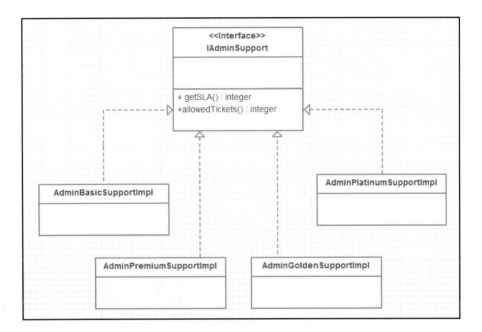

Now, the code to instantiate different classes of the support type can be rewritten as follows:

```
IAdminSupport support = null;

if(Account.supportType__c == 'AdminBasic')
{
   support = new AdminBasicSupportImpl();
}else if(Account.supportType__c == 'AdminPremier')
{
   support = new AdminPremiumSupportImpl();
}else if(Account.supportType__c == 'AdminGold')
{
   support = new AdminGoldSupportImpl();
}else{
   support = new AdminPlatinumSupportImpl();
}

System.debug('Support SLA is - '+support.getSLA());
```

There is no switch-case statement in Apex, and that's why multiple if and else statements are written. According to the product team, a new compiler may be released in 2016 with full support. You can vote for this idea at `https://success.salesforce.com/ideaView?id=087300000 00BrSIAA0`.

As we can see, the preceding code is minimized to create a required instance of a concrete class, and then uses an interface to access methods. This concept is known as **program to interface** and is one of the most often recommended OOP principles suggested to be followed. As interfaces are kinds of contracts, we already know which methods will be implemented by concrete classes, and we can completely rely on the interface to call them, which hides their complex implementation and logic. It has a lot of advantages and a few of them are loose coupling and dependency injection. We have already discussed interfaces and design principles in the previous chapter.

A **concrete class** is a complete class that can be used to instantiate objects. Any class that is not abstract or an interface can be considered a concrete class.

We still have one problem in the previous approach. The code to instantiate concrete classes is still present at many locations and will still require changes if a new support type is added. If we can delegate the creation of concrete classes to some other class, then our code will be completely independent of the existing code and new support types.

This concept of delegating creation of similar types of classes is known as the **factory method pattern**.

The following class can be used to create concrete classes and will act as a factory:

```
/**
 * This factory class is used to instantiate concrete class
 * of respective support type
 * */
public class AdminSupportFactory {
  public static IAdminSupport getInstance(String supporttype){
    IAdminSupport support = null;
    if(supporttype == 'AdminBasic')
    {
      support = new AdminBasicSupportImpl();
    }else if(supporttype == 'AdminPremier')
    {
      support = new AdminPremiumSupportImpl();
    }else if(supporttype == 'AdminGold')
    {
```

```
      support = new AdminGoldSupportImpl();
   }else if(supporttype == 'AdminPlatinum')
   {
      support = new AdminPlatinumSupportImpl();
   }
   return support ;
  }
}
```

In the preceding code, we only need to call the `getInstance(string)` method, and this method will take a decision and return the actual implementation. As return type is an interface, we already know the methods that are defined and we can use the method without actually knowing its implementation. This is a very good example of abstraction.

The final class diagram of the factory method pattern that we discussed will look like this:

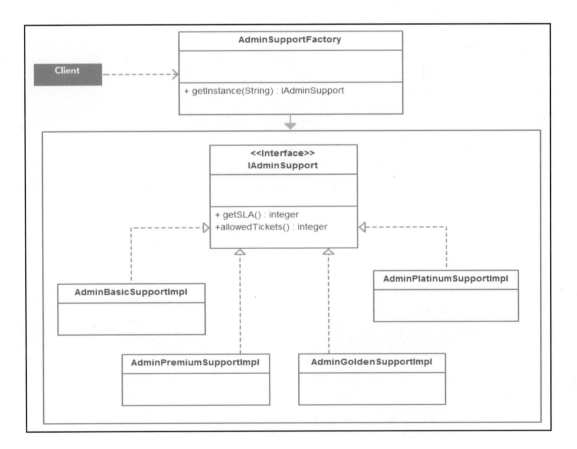

The following code snippet can be used repeatedly by any client code to instantiate a class of any support type:

```
IAdminSupport support = AdminSupportFactory.getInstance ('AdminBasic');
System.debug('Support SLA is - '+support.getSLA());
Output : Support SLA is - 40
```

Reflection in Apex

The problem with the preceding design is that whenever a new support type needs to be added, we need to add a condition to AdminSupportFactory.

We can store the mapping between a support type and its concrete class name in custom setting. This way, whenever a new concrete class is added, we don't even need to change the factory class , only add a new entry to custom setting.

Consider custom setting created by the Support_Type__c name with the Class_Name__c field name of the text type with the following records:

Name	Class name
AdminBasic	AdminBasicSupportImpl
AdminGolden	AdminGoldSupportImpl
AdminPlatinum	AdminPlatinumSupportImpl
AdminPremier	AdminPremiumSupportImpl

However, using reflection, the AdminSupportFactory class can also be rewritten to instantiate service types at runtime as follows:

```
/**
 * This factory class is used to instantiate concrete class
 * of respective support type
 * */
public class AdminSupportFactory {
  public static IAdminSupport getInstance(String supporttype)
  {
    //Read Custom setting to get actual class name on basis of Support type
    Support_Type__c supportTypeInfo =
Support_Type__c.getValues(supporttype);
    //from custom setting get appropriate class name
    Type t = Type.forName(supportTypeInfo.Class_Name__c);
    IAdminSupport retVal = (IAdminSupport)t.newInstance();
```

```
      return retVal;
   }
}
```

In the preceding code, we are using the `Type` system class. This is a very powerful class used to instantiate a new class at runtime. It has the following two important methods:

- `forName`: This returns a type that is equivalent to a passed string
- `newInstance`: This creates a new object for a specified type

Inspecting classes, methods, and variables at runtime without knowing a class name, or instantiating a new object and invoking methods at runtime is known as **reflection** in computer science.

Apex does not support full reflection and only supports a subset of it. This is a very handy and useful feature supported by many programming languages; you can vote for this idea to get it implemented at `https://su ccess.salesforce.com/ideaView?id=08730000000BVaAAK`.

One more advantage of using the factory method, custom setting, and reflection together is that if in future one of the support types needs to be replaced by another service type permanently, then we only need to change the appropriate mapping in custom setting without any code change.

Abstract factory pattern

The Universal Call Center company is growing very fast, and they have a small Force.com application where agents can log a request to place an order for a new computer. Developers have just learned about the factory method design pattern and are very excited to implement the same design pattern in this scenario as well. They decided to create an interface of the computer type and its different implementations, such as *high-configuration* and *low-configuration* computers. However, they were disappointed when they heard that they need to support various types of configurations other than low and high configurations. For example, some computers need high end processors but small monitors and less storage. There were a few requests regarding an average processor but an LCD monitor and SSD storage.

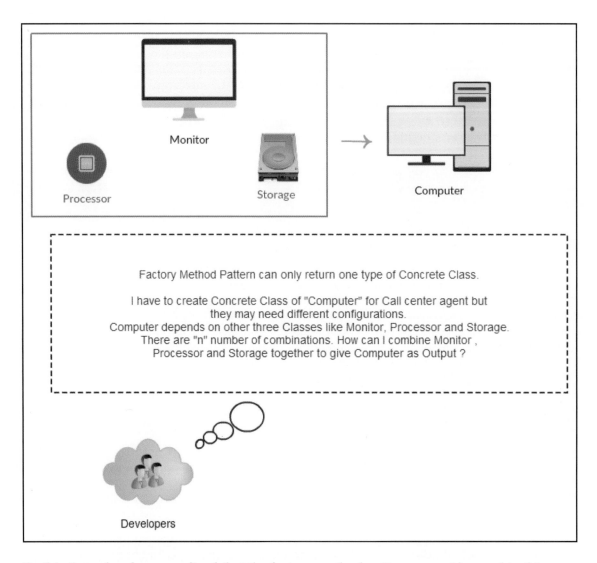

By this time, developers realized that the factory method pattern cannot be used in this scenario. Let's see how they solved this problem.

The abstract factory pattern is used to return a set of factories that when combined together represents a related product. Unlike the factory method pattern, which returns a concrete class, the abstract factory pattern returns another factory. This pattern is used to produce one big functionality by combining many factories.

The provides a way to encapsulate a group of individual factories that have a common theme without depending on concrete classes.

Let's start with processors. Every processor performs the CPU operation with a difference in speed. We can create an interface that can be implemented by all concrete classes, as shown in the following code snippet:

```
interface IProcessor{ void performOperation(); }

class HighEndProcessor implements IProcessor{
public void performOperation(){
System.debug('Super fast Processor');
}
}

class AverageProcessor implements IProcessor{
 public void performOperation(){
System.debug('Average Speed Processor');
}
}
```

In the same way, every hard disk is used to perform a storage operation:

```
interface IStorage {void storeData(); }

class SSDStorage implements IStorage{
  public void storeData(){
    System.debug('Storage Operation is performed in Solid State Drive');
  }
}
class HDDStorage implements IStorage{
  public void storeData(){
    System.debug('Storage Operation is performed on HDD');
  }
}
```

A monitor can have the following structure:

```
interface IMonitor {void display(); }


class LEDMonitor implements IMonitor{
        public void display(){
            System.debug('Display in 17inch LED Monitor');
        }
    }
class LCDMonitor implements IMonitor{
        public void display(){
```

```
            System.debug(Display in LCD Monitor');
        }
    }
```

Until this point, we have different concrete classes for a monitor, storage, and processor. As an extra step, we can create factory classes as well, which will return appropriate concrete classes. However, to assemble a computer, we need to combine all the three factories to produce one result. A computer may be of the `HighPerformance` or `StandardConfiguration` type, which will have different combinations of a monitor, storage, and processor.

We can come up with an interface, which can be implemented by all factory classes of a computer:

```
interface IComputerFactory {
    IProcessor getProcessor();
    IStorage getStorage();
    IMonitor getMonitor();
}
public class HighPerformance implements IComputerFactory{
    public IProcessor getProcessor(){
        return new Quadcore();
    }
    public IStorage getStorage(){
        return new SSDStorage();
    }
    public IMonitor getMonitor(){
        return new LEDMonitor();
    }
}
public class StandardConfiguration implements IComputerFactory{
    public virtual IProcessor getProcessor(){
        return new DualCore();
    }
    public virtual IStorage getStorage(){
        return new HDDStorage();
    }
    public virtual IMonitor getMonitor(){
        return new LCDMonitor();
    }
}
```

We have two factory classes that produce computers by combining the other three factories. The last part is to assemble a computer from all these factories, which can be used by any client application.

Programming languages, such as Java or C# provide you with the concept of a package and namespace, respectively. This is a very useful technique used to organize all related sets of classes at the same place. Unfortunately, Apex doesn't offer this functionality. However, we can mimic it up to some extent using the **inner class**, also known as the **Apex nested class**.

 Java developers can think of an Apex inner class as equivalent to a static nested class. As an inner class is a static class, it cannot access instance members of an outer class directly.

The following code snippet uses an Apex nested class to show how we can organize all the related code discussed till now:

```apex
public class AbstractFactory {
    interface IProcessor{ void performOperation(); }
    interface IStorage {void storeData(); }
    interface IMonitor {void display(); }
        class LEDMonitor implements IMonitor{
          public void display(){
              System.debug('Display in 17inch LED Monitor');
          }

        }
class LCDMonitor implements IMonitor{
        public void display(){
            System.debug('Display in LCD Monitor');
        }

    }

class SSDStorage implements IStorage{
        public void storeData(){
            System.debug('Storage Operation is performed in
                    Solid State Drive');
        }

    }
class HDDStorage implements IStorage{
        public void storeData(){
            System.debug('Storage Operation is performed on HDD');
        }

    }
```

```
class QuadCore implements IProcessor{
    public void performOperation(){
        System.debug('Super fast Processor');
    }

}
class DualCore implements IProcessor{
    public void performOperation(){
        System.debug('Average Speed Processor');
    }

}

public interface IComputerFactory {
  IProcessor getProcessor();
  IStorage getStorage();
  IMonitor getMonitor();

}
public class HighPerformance implements IComputerFactory{
    public IProcessor getProcessor(){
        return new Quadcore();
    }
    public IStorage getStorage(){
        return new SSDStorage();
    }
    public IMonitor getMonitor(){
        return new LEDMonitor();
    }

}
public class StandardConfiguration implements IComputerFactory{
    public virtual IProcessor getProcessor(){
        return new DualCore();
    }
    public virtual IStorage getStorage(){
        return new HDDStorage();
    }
    public virtual IMonitor getMonitor(){
        return new LCDMonitor();
    }

}
public class AssembleComputer
{
    IComputerFactory computer ;
    public AssembleComputer(IComputerFactory comp)
    {
```

```
        computer = comp;
    }
    public void testCompleteSystem()
    {
        IProcessor processor = computer.getProcessor();
        IStorage storage = computer.getStorage();
        IMonitor monitor = computer.getMonitor();
        processor.performOperation();
        storage.storeData();
        monitor.display();
    }

    }

}
```

As you can see, all the related interfaces, concrete classes, and factory classes are part of one class called AbstractFactory; and therefore, the code is easy to maintain.

An example of code snippets used by a client application (an anonymous Apex in the developer console) is as follows:

```
AbstractFactory.IComputerFactory std = new
AbstractFactory.StandardConfiguration();
AbstractFactory.AssembleComputer finalProduct = new
AbstractFactory.AssembleComputer(std);
finalProduct.testCompleteSystem();
```

The output will be as follows:

```
Average Speed Processor
Storage Operation is performed on HDD
Display in LCD Monitor
```

The following class diagram shows you the structure of the abstract factory pattern used in the code:

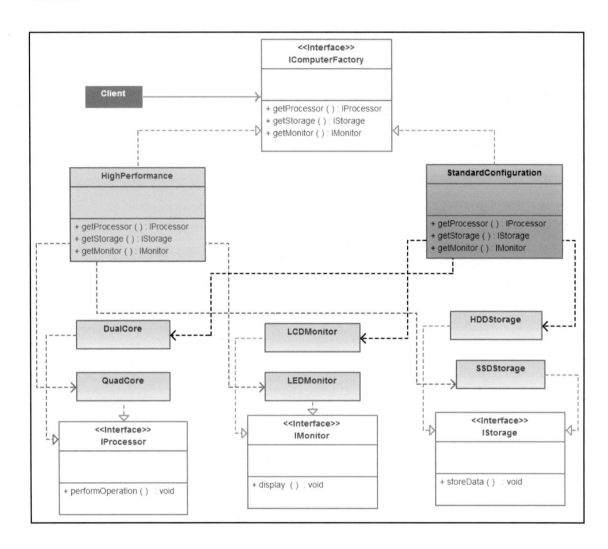

A new perspective on the abstract factory pattern

In the preceding diagram, the `HighPerformance` and `StandardConfigurations` factory classes are tightly coupled and dependent on concrete classes of a processor, monitor, and storage. We can adopt the principle of a previously discussed design pattern, which is the factory method, to add a factory of each type and delegate the object creation to those classes. Currently, the `HighPerformance` and `StandardConfiguration` classes are responsible for instantiating a processor, monitor, and storage.

Let's redesign the preceding solution to add one additional layer of factory methods. In this approach, we cannot use nested Apex classes for concrete classes because nested classes cannot have static methods. So, we will have to create each concrete class as a top-level class.

To make a program as loosely coupled as possible, we need to create a factory class to instantiate concrete classes so that the client class can be independent of instantiating objects:

```
/**
*  Factory class to return actual implementation of Processors
*/
public class ProcessorFactroy{
    //Factory method to return instance of concrete class of processor
    public static IProcessor getInstance(String processorType){
        IProcessor retVal = null;
        if(processorType == 'QuadCore'){
            retVal = new QuadCore();
        }else if(processorType == 'DualCore'){
            retVal = new DualCore();
        }
        return retVal;
    }
}
```

The preceding code snippet uses the Apex reflection to instantiate the class at runtime. In the same way, we need two more factory classes for a monitor and storage, as shown in the following code snippet:

```
/**
 *   Factory class to return actual implementation of Monitors
 */
public class MonitorFactory{
  //Factory method to return instance of concrete class of monitor
  public static IMonitor getInstance(String monitorType){
      IMonitor retVal = null;
      if(monitorType == 'LEDMonitor'){
```

```
                    retVal = new LEDMonitor();
                }else if(monitorType == 'LCDMonitor'){
                    retVal = new LCDMonitor();
                }
                return retVal;
        }
    }


    /**
        *   Factory class to return actual implementation of Storage
        */
    public class StorageFactory{
        //Factory method to return instance of concrete class of Storage
        public static IStorage getInstance(String storageName){
            IStorage retVal = null;
            if(storageName == 'SSDStorage'){
                retVal = new SSDStorage();
            }else if(storageName == 'HDDStorage'){
                retVal = new HDDStorage();
            }
            return retVal;
        }
    }
```

To assemble a computer, we need to combine all three factories to produce one result. A computer may be of the HighPerformance or StandardConfiguration type, which will have different combinations of a monitor, storage, and processor.

We can use the same IComputerFactory interface here as well and implement that factory:

```
Public class HighPerformanceConfiguration implements IComputerFactory{

        public IProcessor getProcessor(){
            return ProcessorFactory.getInstance('QuadCore');
        }

        public IStorage getStorage(){
            return StorageFactory.getInstance('SSDStorage');
        }

        public IMonitor getMonitor(){
            return MonitorFactory.getInstance('LEDMonitor');
        }

    }

  public class StandardConfiguration implements IComputerFactory{
```

```
        public IProcessor getProcessor(){
            return ProcessorFactory.getInstance('DualCore');
        }

        public IStorage getStorage(){
            return StorageFactory.getInstance('HDDStorage');
        }

        public IMonitor getMonitor(){
            return MonitorFactory.getInstance('LCDMonitor');
        }


    }
```

We have two factory classes (`HighPerformanceConfiguration`
and `StandardConfiguration`) that produce a computer by combining the other three
factories. The only part remaining is to assemble a computer from all of these factories,
which can be used by any client application:

```
public class AssembleComputer
{
    IComputerFactory computer ;
    IProcessor processor ;
    IStorage storage ;
    IMonitor monitor ;
    /**
     * Constructor to instantiate all factories
     * */
    public AssembleComputer(IComputerFactory comp)
    {
        computer = comp;
        processor = computer.getProcessor();
        storage = computer.getStorage();
        monitor = computer.getMonitor();
    }
    /**
     * run test to see if all factories are assembled together
     * */
    public void runSystemDiagnosis()
    {
        processor.performOperation();
        storage.storeData();
        monitor.display();
    }
}
```

The examples of code snippets used by a client application are as follows.

Snippet 1:

```
IComputerFactory highConfig = new HighPerformanceConfiguration();

AssembleComputer highConfig_Computer = new AssembleComputer(highConfig);

highConfig_Computer.runSystemDiagnosis();
```

When the preceding code snippet is executed, you'll get the following output:

```
Super fast Processor
Storage Operation is performed in Solid State Drive
Display in 17inch LED Monitor
```

Snippet 2:

```
IComputerFactory stdConfig = new StandardConfiguration();

AssembleComputer stdConfig_Computer = new AssembleComputer(stdConfig);

stdConfig_Computer.runSystemDiagnosis();
```

When the preceding code snippet is executed, you'll get the following output:

```
Average Speed Processor
Storage Operation is performed on HDD
Display in LCD Monitor
```

An updated class diagram will look like the following image. We have introduced an extra layer of factory classes to handle the creation of a processor, storage, and monitor:

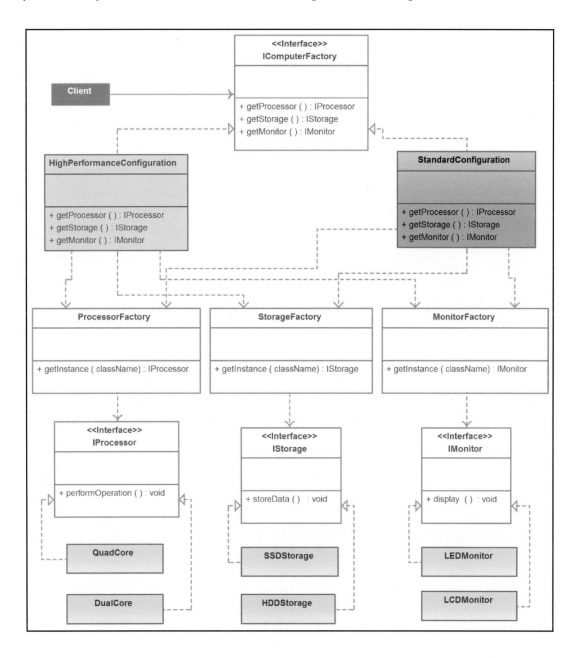

In this design, we learned how multiple factories can be combined together without knowing their actual implementation to produce a final product.

The singleton pattern

The **singleton design pattern** restricts the instantiation of a class to only one object.

This is a useful design pattern in Apex and is frequently used. As discussed in the previous chapter, Salesforce has various governor limits; for example, a number of SOQL queries, a number of query rows returned, and a number of DML operations that can be performed in a single request.

Using the singleton design pattern, we can make sure that utility classes are instantiated only once, which can help in avoiding governor limits.

The sales division of a call center receives calls either from a customer or broker who is interested in the product. If a call comes directly from a customer, then the call center agents need to create a new opportunity record with all the required information. Alternatively, if a call comes from a broker, then the call center agents need to create an opportunity record and then record it for a broker as well. Brokers are eligible for commission if they sell company products to new customers. The company also has area-specific offices and would like to autopopulate it while creating or updating the opportunity and broker.

Salesforce developers of the call center came up with the following database structure:

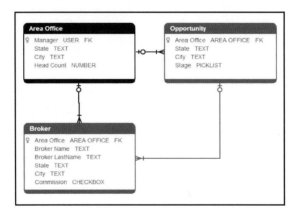

Developers created the following utility class to get the area office saved in the Salesforce object on the basis of its state and city:

```
/**
 * This class is used to query all existing offices and utility methods
 * to return Office record on basis of state and city
 * */
public class AreaOfficeUtil {

    private List<Area_Office__c> lstAllOffices;

    private Map<String,Area_Office__c> mpAllOffices ;
    public AreaOfficeUtil(){
        //Even though there are no more than 1500 records, but
        //on safer side, Limit 2000
        lstAllOffices = [Select
                            Name,
                            City__c,
                            State__c,
                            Manager__c,
                            Head_Count__c
                        FROM
                            Area_Office__c
                        LIMIT 2000
                        ];
    mpAllOffices = new Map<String,Area_Office__c>();
     for(Area_Office__c ofc : lstAllOffices){
         mpAllOffices.put(ofc.State__c+'-'+ofc.City__c,ofc);
     }
    }
    //  Get "Area_Office__c" on basis of state and city
    public Area_Office__c getOffice(String state, String city){
        return mpAllOffices.get(state+'-'+city);
    }
}
```

In the preceding class, SOQL is executed in a constructor, and a map of offices is created with state-city as keys so that in all subsequent requests, developers can save SOQL.

Business users wanted to check that whenever an opportunity is created or updated, a call center agent should enter a proper area office, then it needs to be autopopulated. One more requirement was given that if an opportunity is marked as closed won, then the related broker qualifies for commission.

Developers came up with the following trigger on an opportunity:

```
trigger OpportunityTrigger on Opportunity (before insert, before update,
after update) {
    // Instance of utility class to perform Area office
    // related operations
    AreaOfficeUtil util = new AreaOfficeUtil();
```

```
    //This set will hold Id of all closed won Opportunities
    Set<Id> setClosedWonOpp = new Set<Id>();
    for(Opportunity opp : Trigger.New)
    {
        //Make sure Opportunity should not be tried to be
        // updated in after trigger, else we will get
        // "record read only" error

        if(!Trigger.isAfter)
        {
            //If Area Office field is not populated and
            //state, city is valued

            if(opp.Area_Office__c == null && opp.State__c != null &&
opp.City__c != null )
            {
                Area_Office__c ofc = util.getOffice(opp.State__c,
opp.City__c);
                if(ofc != null)
                {
                    opp.Area_Office__c = ofc.Id;
                }
            }
        }
        //If Opportunity is closed won then update all related brokers
qualified for commission

        if(opp.StageName == 'Closed Won' && Trigger.isAfter &&
Trigger.isUpdate){
            setClosedWonOpp.add(opp.Id);
        }
    }
    //Save SOQL if there set is empty
    if(!setClosedWonOpp.isEmpty())
    {
        List<Broker__c> lstBrokersToUpdate = [
                Select
                        Id,
                        Commision__c,
                        Opportunity__c
                FROM
                        Broker__c
                WHERE
                        Opportunity__c IN:setClosedWonOpp ];
        for(Broker__c b : lstBrokersToUpdate)
        {
            b.commission__c = true;
        }
```

```
            //update all qualified brokers at once
            Database.update(lstBrokersToUpdate,false);
    }
}
```

After a few days, the same requirement to autopopulate a broker's area office was given to the developers, and they came up with the following simple trigger:

```
trigger BrokerTrigger on Broker__c (before insert, before update) {

    // Instance of utility class to perform Area office
    // related operations
    AreaOfficeUtil util = new AreaOfficeUtil();
    for(Broker__c b : Trigger.New)
    {
        if(b.Area_Office__c == null && Trigger.isBefore
            && b.State__c != null && b.City__c != null)
        {

            Area_Office__c ofc = util.getOffice(b.State__c, b.City__c);

            if(ofc != null)
            {
                b.Area_Office__c = ofc.Id;
            }
        }
    }
}
```

The code was working fine, as was expected by business users of the call center. Like all software development projects, a day came when the Salesforce technical architect reviewed the code and informed them that the code was not written efficiently. Everyone was surprised as the developers had already tried their best to make the code modular by delegating access of area office to the utility class. The Salesforce technical architect informed them that if an opportunity has one or more brokers, and when an opportunity is moved to closed won, a total of five SOQL queries will be executed and this could be reduced to just two SOQLs.

The Salesforce architect asked the team to go through the order of execution of a trigger. Developers understood the issue. The following image shows the order of execution:

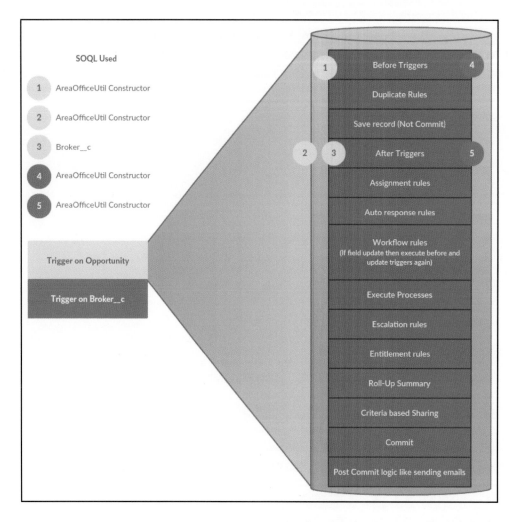

The preceding image does not provide a detailed information of the execution order in Salesforce. To read more about this, refer to https://developer.salesforce.com/docs /atlas.en-us.apexcode.meta/apexcode/apex_triggers_order_of_execution.ht m.

In the preceding image, we can see that a constructor of the AreaOfficeUtil class is using one SOQL query. For the Opportunity record, before and after the event of a trigger creates one instance each of AreaOfficeUtil. Also, as the Opportunity trigger updates the broker record, it results in the invocation of a broker trigger. A broker trigger also creates one instance each of AreaOfficeUtil before and after events. AreaOfficeUtil is instantiated a total of four times, resulting in four SOQL queries.

This is just one example; however, there are many similar situations in the project where the same object is used between different triggers and fires the same SOQL multiple times. As discussed in Chapter 1, *An Introduction to Apex Design Pattern*, Salesforce is a multi-tenant platform, and it forces many governor limits to avoid the monopoly of resources. One of the most common governor limits that Apex developers should be wary of is the total number of SOQL queries used in a single user request.

One of the Salesforce developers had an idea and changed the AreaOfficeUtil class, as shown in the following code:

```
/**
 * This class is used to query all existing offices and utility methods
 * to return Office record on basis of state and city
 * */
public class AreaOfficeUtil {

    private List<Area_Office__c> lstAllOffices;

    private Map<String,Area_Office__c> mpAllOffices ;
    //Static variable to hold instance of same class
    //and avoid creation of object again

    private static AreaOfficeUtil selfInstance = null;
    //Static method to check if its already instantiated,
    //if not then call private constructor and return
    //object

    public static AreaOfficeUtil getInstance(){

        if(selfInstance == null)
            selfInstance = new AreaOfficeUtil();

        return selfInstance;
    }
    //Private constructor to make sure no one
    //can instantiate this class

    private AreaOfficeUtil(){
        //Even though there are no more than 1500 records, but
```

```
                    //on safer side, Limit 2000
                    lstAllOffices = [Select
                                    Name,
                                    City__c,
                                    State__c,
                                    Manager__c,
                                    Head_Count__c
                                FROM
                                    Area_Office__c
                                LIMIT 2000
                                ];
            mpAllOffices = new Map<String,Area_Office__c>();
            for(Area_Office__c ofc : lstAllOffices){

                mpAllOffices.put(ofc.State__c+'-'+ofc.City__c,ofc);

            }
        }
        // Get "Area_Office__c" on basis of state and city
        public Area_Office__c getOffice(String state, String city){

            return mpAllOffices.get(state+'-'+city);

        }
    }
```

In the `Opportunity` and `Broker__c` triggers, we need to change the following line of code:

```
AreaOfficeUtil util = new AreaOfficeUtil();
```

This line is changed to:

```
AreaOfficeUtil util = AreaOfficeUtil.getInstance();
```

The preceding code provides a good usage of private constructors.

Private constructors

Private constructors are special types of constructors. They are used to restrict other classes to instantiate objects, and the only way to instantiate is inside a class itself. In most scenarios, the `Static` method is exposed to instantiate it from an external class.

The idea was that the `Opportunity` trigger and `Broker` trigger were executed in a single request. So, the `AreaOfficeUtil` class will be instantiated only once during the entire user request cycle. This will result in only one SOQL query getting invoked. The Salesforce static variable solved this purpose.

Unlike a static variable in Java where it lasts until the JVM runs, the Salesforce static variable scope exists only in one transaction/request.

The following image shows a class diagram of the singleton pattern used in the previous example:

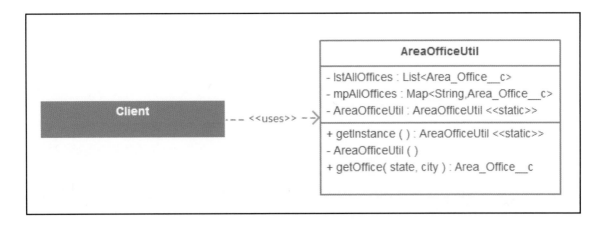

The builder pattern

The **builder pattern** is used to instantiate an object of a complex class using the step-by-step approach and return a constructed object at once.

The intention of the factory method and abstract factory method patterns is to use polymorphism to construct objects, as discussed in the initial part of this book. However, in this design pattern, a new independent `Builder` class is used to construct objects. This pattern is very useful when many parameters are needed to construct and initialize an object.

Developers of Universal Call Center were enjoying their success after the implementation of the singleton pattern and resolving excess SOQL queries. Now, it was time to write a test class for the code written in the singleton design pattern.

Developers came up with the following test class:

```
@isTest(SeeAllData = false)
public class OpportunityTriggerTest {
    //Test method to test if state is populated
```

```
    //on Opportunity and Brokers
    static testMethod void validateState()
    {
        //create user record so that it can be used while
        //creating Area office records
        Profile p = [SELECT Id FROM Profile WHERE Name='Standard User'];
        //Use Crypto.getRandomInteger() to get random
        //string to make sure username is unique
        User u = new User(
            Alias = 'standt',
            Email='dummyEmail@email.com',
            EmailEncodingKey='UTF-8',
            LastName='Testing',
            LanguageLocaleKey='en_US',
            LocaleSidKey='en_US',
            ProfileId = p.Id,
            TimeZoneSidKey='America/Los_Angeles',
            UserName='dummyEmail'+Crypto.getRandomInteger()+'@email.com');
        insert u;
        Area_Office__c ofc = new Area_Office__c(
            Manager__c = u.Id,
            State__c = 'CT',
            City__c = 'Manchester');
        insert ofc ;
      Opportunity opp = new Opportunity(
            Name = 'Test Opportunity Test',
            CloseDate = Date.today().addDays(7),
            StageName = 'Prospecting',
            State__c = 'CT',
            City__c = 'Manchester'
        ) ;

        //Reset governor limits while Saving Opportunity
        Test.startTest();
        insert opp;
        //If there is any asynchornous process
        //stoptest() will make sure its executed
        Test.stopTest();
        //Get inserted record from Table to assert
        //Area_Office lookup
        Opportunity oppInserted = [SELECT Area_Office__c FROM Opportunity
Where Id=:opp.Id];
        //Confirm that Area office lookup is not blank
        System.assertNotEquals(oppInserted.Area_Office__c, null) ;
    }
}
```

Test classes

Unlike other programming languages, overall, 75% of the code coverage is mandatory in Salesforce before the code is deployed to production. Other than the mandatory code coverage, every trigger should have some code coverage else the deployment will fail.

To read more about test classes, you can refer to the Salesforce documentation at `https://developer.salesforce.com/docs/atlas.en-us.apexcode.meta/apexcode/apex_qs_test.htm`.

We can run the preceding test in the developer console by navigating to **Test** | **New Run** | **Select Tests** | **OpportunityTriggerTest** | **Run**.

After running the test class, the developer console displays that the `Test` method has passed successfully and they need to write some more test cases for negative and bulk scenarios. Even though the `Test` method was executed successfully, developers were not satisfied, because in the preceding code, out of around 60 lines only 2-3 lines were actually used to validate the output of the code; the remaining lines were all about creating test data.

Creating the test data involves multiple steps, such as creating a user, area office, and actual `Opportunity` record. Also, this test was written to test the `Opportunity` trigger; in the future, they need to write a test class for a `Broker` trigger. To create the test data for a `Broker` test class, all the code for the `Opportunity` creation will be needed in addition to the code required to create a `Broker` record.

Developers started brainstorming on how they can make the test data creation code more reusable and consistent across an application.

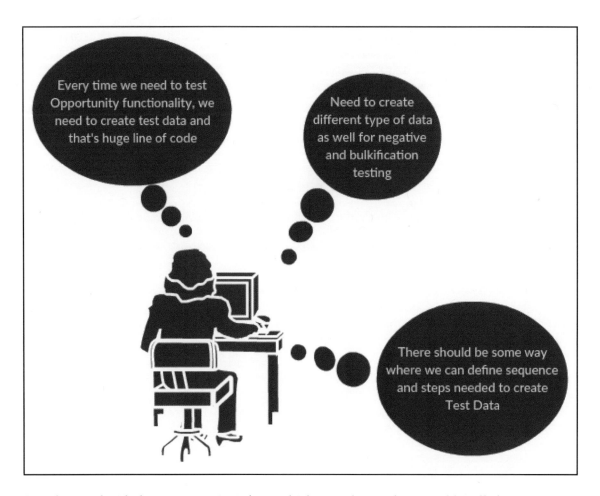

Developers decided to create an interface, which must be implemented by all classes, to build the test data for the Opportunity object:

```
public interface IOppTestDataBuilder {
    //Insert manager record
    void createManager();
    //Insert Area office with manager field populated
    void createAreaOffice();
    //Create Opportunity but do not insert it
    void createOpportunity();
    //return created opportunity
    Opportunity getOpportunity();

}
```

Then, they created the following concrete class, which implements the preceding interface, to create an opportunity with a valid relationship with area office:

```
@isTest
public class OppTestData_ValidOfficeImpl implements IOppTestDataBuilder {
    public Opportunity opp;
    private User u;
    private Area_Office__c aofc;
    public void createManager(){
        //create user record so that it can be used while
        //creating Area office records
        Profile p = [SELECT Id FROM Profile WHERE Name='Standard User'];
        //Use Crypto.getRandomInteger() to get random
        //string to make sure username is unique
            u = new User(
            Alias = 'standt',
            Email='dummyEmail@email.com',
            EmailEncodingKey='UTF-8',
            LastName='Testing',
            LanguageLocaleKey='en_US',
            LocaleSidKey='en_US',
            ProfileId = p.Id,
            TimeZoneSidKey='America/Los_Angeles',
            UserName='dummyEmail'+Crypto.getRandomInteger()+'@email.com');
        insert u;
    }
    public void createAreaOffice(){
        Area_Office__c ofc = new Area_Office__c(
            Manager__c = u.Id,
            State__c = 'CT',
            City__c = 'Manchester');
        insert ofc ;
    }
    public void createOpportunity(){
        opp = new Opportunity(
          Name = 'Test Opportunity Test',
           CloseDate = Date.today().addDays(7),
          StageName = 'Prospecting',
          State__c = 'CT',
          City__c = 'Manchester'
        ) ;
    }
    public Opportunity getOpportunity(){
        return opp;
    }

}
```

You must have noticed that the preceding class is marked with the `@isTest` annotation. One of the advantages of marking a class with the `@isTest` annotation is that it will not count against the organization limit of Apex classes. As this class is going to be used only in `TestMethods`, it makes sense to mark it with this annotation. You can read more about `@isTest` from the Salesforce documentation at `https://developer.sal esforce.com/docs/atlas.en-us.apexcode.meta/apexcode/apex_ classes_annotation_isTest.htm`.

So far, we have a concrete class, which is also known as the **builder class**, that performs all distinct operations to create new `Opportunity` and related records.

However, it is vital to maintain the sequence of the method execution. For example, in the preceding scenario, the `createManager()` method should run before the `createAreaOffice()` method. In view of this separation of concerns, we will build a new class to maintain the sequence of execution of builder class methods, and this class is referred to as the **director class** as per the builder pattern:

```
@isTest
public class OppTestData_Director {
    public Opportunity Construct(IOppTestDataBuilder oppBuilder)
    {
        oppBuilder.createManager();

        oppBuilder.createAreaOffice();

        oppBuilder.createOpportunity();

        return oppBuilder.getOpportunity();

    }

}
```

Now, we can rewrite our test class using the builder pattern:

```
@isTest
public class OpportunityTrigger_BuilderPattern_Test {
    static testMethod void validateState()
    {
        //Use Builder Pattern to create Opportunity Data
        oppTestData_Director director = new oppTestData_Director();
        Opportunity opp =  director.Construct(new
OppTestData_ValidOfficeImpl()) ;
        Test.startTest();
        insert opp;
```

```
        Test.stopTest();
        Opportunity oppInserted = [SELECT Area_Office__c FROM Opportunity
    Where Id=:opp.Id];
        //Confirm that Area office lookup is not blank
        System.assertNotEquals(oppInserted.Area_Office__c, null) ;
    }
}
```

The following image depicts the class diagram of the builder pattern used earlier:

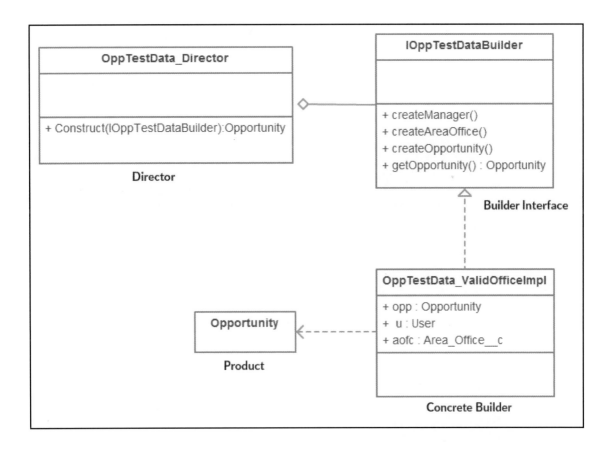

The difference between the abstract factory method and the builder pattern

Sometimes, it may seem confusing to understand the difference between the abstract factory method and the builder pattern. In the abstract factory pattern example, as mentioned earlier, we assembled a computer from different parts such as a monitor, hard disk, and storage. You may think that the builder pattern could also be a good solution for this problem and may work well. It is all about what fits in a given situation. The following are some high-level differences between the abstract factory and builder patterns:

The builder pattern	The abstract factory pattern
This focuses on constructing a complex object step by step	This emphasizes a family of product objects (either simple or complex)
This returns the product as a final step	In this pattern, the product is returned immediately

Code to auto generate test data

In the preceding design pattern, we discussed how we can solve a problem to generate test data for a particular object. However, you can also create a generic Apex class/method, which can take the SObject type as the input and iterate through all available fields using the Dynamic apex. Once all the fields are retrieved, we can determine which are mandatory fields and generate a record for that sObject with mandatory fields populated with the default values. If you don't want to reinvent wheels, there is a very good open source project named *Smart Factory for Force.com* available at GitHub, which can provide you with a good start toward implementing this functionality. It will definitely save a lot of time and effort when writing the code to generate dummy records. The GitHub repository can be found at https://github.com/mbotos/SmartFactory-for-Force.com.

The prototype pattern

The prototype design pattern is used to create a new object of a class based on an existing object of the same class. It helps avoid the repetitive code used to initialize a newly created object.

Developers of Universal Call Center solved many problems associated with the creation of an object, using design patterns, such as the factory method, singleton, abstract factory method, and builder pattern. Now, they are confident about how to simplify, manage, and solve problems created while instantiating objects. They were working on the module of an application where they needed to create a duplicate copy of the Apex helper class used to perform various operations.

The following is a code snippet of a wrapper class, which simply sets and gets the `Opportunity` object:

```
public class OpportunityWrapper {
    private Opportunity opp ;
    public void setOpportunity(Opportunity o){
        opp = o ;
    }
    public Id getOpportunityId()
    {
        return opp != null ? opp.Id : null ;
    }
    //Some other utility methods
    //related to Opportunity record
    //...
}
```

A developer needs a copy of this wrapper class as it has many other properties, which are computed on the basis of a user action. If they use a new keyword, it will create a completely new instance of an object, and every variable will be initialized with default values.

A user tried the following code in the developer console and tried to check the debug log to see how the clone method would work in Apex:

```
Opportunity opp = [SELECT ID,Name,StageName, CloseDate FROM Opportunity
Limit 1];
OpportunityWrapper wr = new OpportunityWrapper();
wr.setOpportunity(opp);

//clone existing wrapper class
OpportunityWrapper clonedWrapper = wr.clone();
```

```
System.debug('Actual Opp Name Before Clone - '+opp.Name);

//Change name of newly cloned Opp
clonedWrapper.setOpportunityName('Cloned Opp');
System.debug('Actual Opp Name After Clone Change -'+opp.Name);
System.debug('Cloned Opp Name - '+clonedWrapper.getOpportunityName());
```

Output:

```
 Actual Opp Name Before Clone - GenePoint Standby Generator
Actual Opp Name After Clone Change -Cloned Opp
Cloned Opp Name - Cloned Opp
```

We can clearly see what's happening here. Normally, when we say clone, it means copy all values from a source (`wr`) to a target object (`clonedWrapper`), and any operation on the target object should not have any impact on the source object. In this case, changing a target object's opportunity name is like changing the source object's opportunity name as well. This is known as a **shallow copy clone**.

The shallow and deep clone

OOPs-based platforms generally have two types of memories: the stack and heap memory. All custom datatypes (objects) are saved in a heap memory, and primitive datatypes and instance variables (objects' reference) are saved in a stack memory.

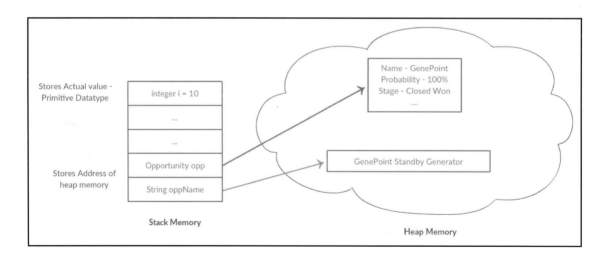

In the preceding image, we can see that primitive data types, such as integers, are saved in a stack memory; however, in case of a complex or custom data type, only the address of a heap memory is saved in a stack memory. A string is also considered as a nonprimitive data type and, therefore, it's actually stored in the heap memory.

 In a situation when more than one variable points to the same object in memory is known as aliasing. You can read more about it at `https://en.wikipedia.org/wiki/Aliasing_(computing)`.

When we create a shallow clone of an object, an initial and cloned object refer to the same object in a heap memory, as shown in the following diagram:

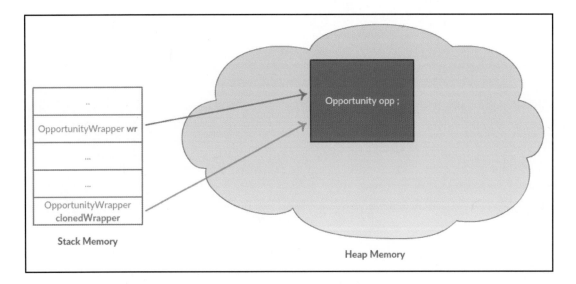

When we create a deep clone of an object, then a new copy of an initial object is created in a heap memory and referred by a cloned object.

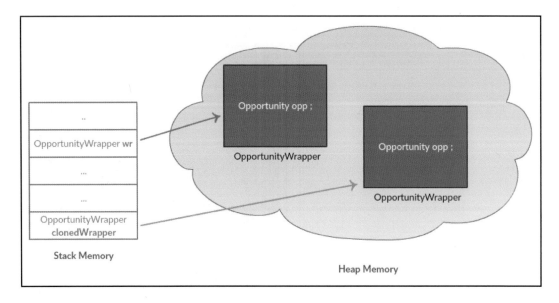

Before making any code changes, developers realized that this is a very common situation where they need a deep clone of an object instead of a shallow clone.

Every Apex class needs to be cloned differently depending on the member types in a class. So, developers came up with an interface, which needs to be implemented by every Apex class that requires a clone feature:

```
public interface IClone {
    IClone cloneObject();
}
```

The return type of the `cloneObject()` method is declared as `IClone`. The preceding class can be rewritten as follows:

```
public class OpportunityWrapper implements IClone{
    private Opportunity opp ;
    public void setOpportunity(Opportunity o){
        opp = o ;
    }
    public String getOpportunityName()
    {
        return opp != null ? opp.Name : '' ;
    }
    public void setOpportunityName(String Name)
    {
      if(opp != null)
```

```
        opp.Name = Name ;
    }

    //Implement CloneObject() method from interface "IClone"
    public IClone cloneObject(){

        //Current Apex Class type
        OpportunityWrapper clonedObject = new OpportunityWrapper();

        //Use Clone() method of SObject
        Opportunity clonedOpp = opp.clone(false,false,false,false);
        clonedObject.setOpportunity(clonedOpp) ;
        return clonedObject;
    }
}
```

 There is one more approach frequently followed by Salesforce developers to clone a complete Apex class, which is by serializing it as JSON and then deserializing it back to an appropriate Apex class type.

The Clone() method is exposed by sObject and hence available to all standard and custom objects of Salesforce. The following code is a signature and definition of all parameters of the Clone() method:

```
public sObject clone(Boolean preserveId, Boolean isDeepClone, Boolean
preserveReadonlyTimestamps, BooleanpreserveAutonumber)
```

A brief description of the parameters used in the preceding code snippet is as follows:

- preserveId: This determines whether the ID of the original object is preserved or cleared in the duplicate. If set to true, the ID is copied to the duplicate. The default value is false, which means that the ID is cleared.
- isDeepClone: This determines whether the method creates a complete copy of the sObject field or just a reference.
- preserveReadonlyTimestamps: This determines whether the read-only timestamp fields are preserved or cleared in the duplicate.
- preserveAutonumber: This determines whether an automatic number of fields of the original object are preserved or cleared in the duplicate.

The standard `Clone()` method of Salesforce will copy only those fields of an object that have been previously accessed in SOQL. Let's say in SOQL, we used only the ID and Name field to fetch from an opportunity. Even though an opportunity may have hundreds of fields, only two fields will be copied by the `Clone()` method.

The following image shows the prototype design pattern:

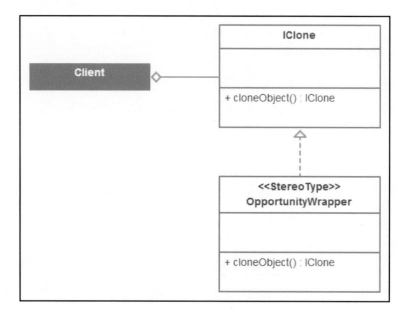

Summary

In this chapter, we discussed how to deal with various situations while instantiating objects using design patterns, such as the factory method, abstract factory method, singleton, builder, and prototype pattern.

The following table shows a summary of the design patterns discussed in this chapter:

Design patterns	Summary
The factory method pattern	This creates objects of the same family of classes.
The abstract factory pattern	This creates a single object consisting of objects of different factories to represent a related product.
The singleton pattern	This restricts to a single instance of a class.
The builder pattern	This hides the complexity and sequence to initialize a complex object.
The prototype pattern	This creates a new object on the basis of an existing object of the same type.

3

Structural Patterns

In the previous chapter, we have seen that creational patterns can help us create objects with a simplified and extensible approach. Moving forward, as we develop various classes, our next challenge is to integrate these classes. In some scenarios, where we need to establish a relationship between two classes and they do not know each other's behavior or are incompatible with each other or are frequently changed, it is very important to establish a robust relationship between these classes. Structural design patterns help us design a robust relationship between multiple classes.

Structural patterns can be used in the following scenarios:

- Dynamically assigning an additional behavior to the existing object
- Creating a relationship between incompatible classes
- Simplifying an interaction with complex classes
- Reusing an object to improve the memory footprint

In this chapter, we will discuss various ways to create an optimum relationship between multiple classes.

We will go through the following structural design patterns:

- The facade pattern
- The adapter pattern
- The bridge pattern
- The composite pattern
- The decorator pattern
- The flyweight pattern

The facade pattern

By the time an application is being built, the chances are high that the existing classes become more complex and require complex client code for interaction. Often, this complex code for interaction is duplicated wherever a relationship is to be established. Also, a developer needs to be aware of all the aspects of this complex interaction code, such as a sequence in which it should be executed. The faÃ§ade pattern helps us hide such complex interaction code and makes it reusable.

 The intention of the **faÃ§ade design pattern** is to convert complex Apex classes into simplified classes or interfaces where groups of classes are either wrapped into one class or only one class is used to delegate responsibilities to the other classes.

Most prominent use cases of the faÃ§ade design pattern include scenarios where a client needs to have multiple interactions to achieve a unit of work or the interaction code is duplicated at multiple locations.

Consider the example of an online shopping store. Whenever any order is placed in such an application, a series of complicated steps need to be executed before a product is shipped to the client address. It needs to go through steps, such as updating the inventory, verifying the address, calculating a discount, verifying payment, and shipping the product. All these steps are complex and can be considered modules. Also, the sequence of these steps is equally important.

Let's take a look at the following code for all the previously mentioned modules of an online store application. Below each Apex class, you will see the steps performed before a product is shipped to the customer:

```
/*
Class to contain methods related to operations on Inventory
*/
public class Inventory {
  //This method updates Inventory
  public boolean updateInventory(String prodId, Integer count)
  {
    System.debug(count+' Product with Id '+prodId+' is subtracted from
Inventory');
    return true;
  }
}

/*
Class to contain methods related to operations on Address Verification
*/
```

```
public class AddressVerification {
  //This method is used to verify address
  public boolean verify(String zipAdd){
    System.debug('Product can be shipped at zip - '+zipAdd);
    return true;
  }
}


/*
Class to contain methods related to operations for applying discount
*/
public class ApplyDiscount {

  //return discounted price
  public decimal calculate(Decimal actualPrice,Decimal discount){
    Decimal finalPrice = actualPrice - (discount/100 *actualPrice) ;
    System.debug('Final price, After '+  discount/100 +'% discount applied
is '+finalPrice);
    return finalPrice;
  }
}

public class PaymentVerification {
    public boolean verify(String cardNumber){
      System.debug('Card with number '+cardNumber+' is used for payment');
      return true;
    }
}


/*
Class to contain methods related to operations for shipping
*/
public class ShipToAddress {
  //Ship product to address
  public boolean ship(String add, String prodName){
    System.debug('"'+prodName+'" is shipped to '+add);
    return true;
  }
}
```

In a real-world application, preceding classes can be huge and can involve numerous transactions. For the sake of simplicity, only a skeleton of classes has been provided in this example.

We need one more class to hold all the information about the product ordered by a customer:

```
public class OrderDetail {
```

```
      //public properties
      public String productId {get;set;}
      public String productName {get;set;}
      public Integer productCount  {get;set;}
      public String zipCode {get;set;}
      public Decimal price {get;set;}
      public Decimal discount {get;set;}
      public String paymentCardNumber {get;set;}
      public String address {get;set;}
      //Constructor
      public OrderDetail(String productId, String productName, Integer
      productCount, String zipCode, Decimal price, Decimal discount,
      String paymentCardNumber, String address ){
        this.productId = productId;
        this.productName = productName;
        this.productCount = productCount;
        this.zipCode = zipCode;
        this.price = price;
        this.discount = discount;
        this.paymentCardNumber = paymentCardNumber;
        this.address = address;
      }
  }
```

Now, to place an order, the following code needs to be used at all the required locations:

```
OrderDetail order = new OrderDetail('IBN-abcd123','Apex Design Pattern', 1,
'06042',40,15,'123456789098754','Manchester Buckland hills');

Inventory inv = new Inventory();
inv.updateInventory(order.productId , order.productCount );

AddressVerification add = new AddressVerification();
add.verify(order.zipCode);

ApplyDiscount disc = new ApplyDiscount();
disc.calculate(order.price , order.discount);

PaymentVerification pym = new PaymentVerification();
pym.verify(order.paymentCardNumber);

ShipToAddress shipProduct = new ShipToAddress();
shipProduct.ship(order.address , order.productName);
```

The output of the preceding code is as follows:

```
1 Product with Id IBN-abcd123 is subtracted from Inventory
Product can be shipped at zip - 06042
```

```
Final price, After 0.15% discount applied is 34.00
Card with number 123456789098754 is used for payment
"Apex Design Pattern" is shipped to Manchester Buckland hills
```

The following figure shows a high-level diagram of the current state of an application:

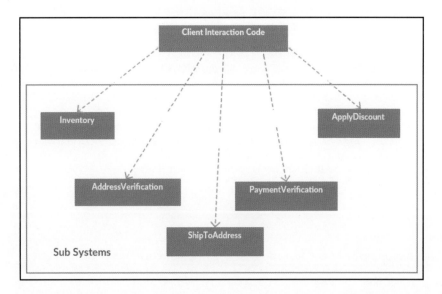

In the preceding example, a problem is very evident. Every piece of client code has to ensure that all the required steps are executed and as per the specified sequence. Any changes made to the steps involved or to the sequence of these steps will result in a ripple effect on all code locations wherever they have been used.

Also, in the preceding figure, the client code is tightly coupled with multiple subsystems, such as card verification, inventory update, applying discount, and so on.

As all the subsystems are well tested and dependent on many other modules, changing the code would not be a wise decision. As there are many large classes, and the client uses the repetitive code for interaction, it strongly hints at the usage of the faÃ§ade pattern.

While implementing faÃ§ade pattern, we do not make any changes to the existing code, but we create a new class or layer, which takes care of the interaction with subsystems.

The following Apex class represents a newly written faÃ§ade class:

```
public class OnlineStoreFacade {
  //This method takes care of processing all steps in sub systems
  public void processSteps(OrderDetail order){

    Inventory inv = new Inventory();
    AddressVerification add = new AddressVerification();
    ApplyDiscount disc = new ApplyDiscount();
    PaymentVerification pym = new PaymentVerification();
    ShipToAddress shipProduct = new ShipToAddress();

    inv.updateInventory(order.productId , order.productCount );
    add.verify(order.zipCode);
    disc.calculate(order.price , order.discount);
    pym.verify(order.paymentCardNumber);
    shipProduct.ship(order.address , order.productName);
  }
}
```

The client needs to use only the following three lines of code for the interaction:

```
OrderDetail order = new OrderDetail('IBN-abcd123','Apex Design Pattern', 1,
'06042',40,15,'123456789098754','Manchester Buckland hills');
OnlineStoreFacade facade = new OnlineStoreFacade();
facade.processSteps(order);
```

The following class diagram shows the faÃ§ade pattern implemented in this example:

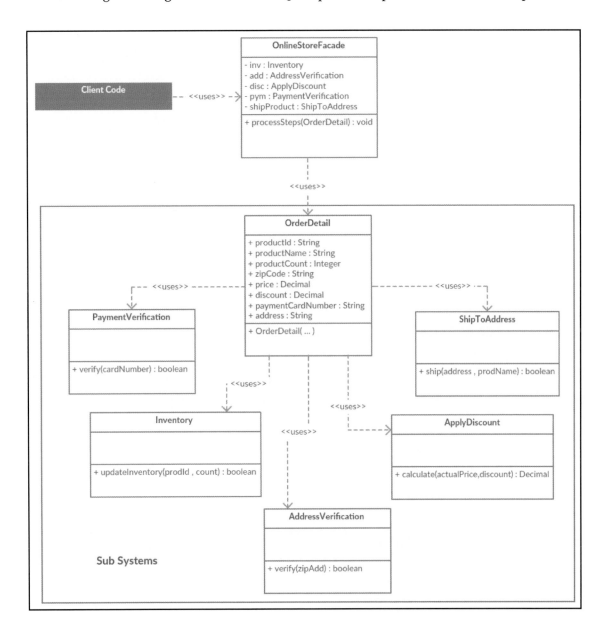

Other use cases

Let's say that we have generated Apex classes from a web service's WSDL file using the WSDLtoApex tool. Each time before invoking a web service, we may need to set up the endpoint URL or timeout or any other parameter. This leads to code redundancy. In these scenarios as well, we can have a common Apex class, which can be used to invoke web services, and all these repetitive settings can be part of this Apex class.

WSDLtoApex is an open source tool and part of the Force.com IDE plugin for Eclipse. You can find this tool, or if you want to contribute to this tool, you can visit its GitHub repository page at `https://github.com/force dotcom/WSDL2Apex`.

There is one more tool available at FuseIT, which goes one level higher by allowing you to generate the Apex class only for the required method from WSDL. This tool is very helpful in scenarios where WSDL generates hundreds of classes and consumes the allowed Apex limit for the Salesforce instance. You can find more information about this tool at `http ://www.fuseit.com/Solutions/SFDC-Explorer.aspx`.

Points to consider

- The faÃ§ade pattern emphasizes on ensuring compatibility with the existing implementations by not modifying the existing classes
- It is widely used in API development to provide easier client interaction

The adapter pattern

The name *adapter* is derived from the real world, wherein we have various adapters being used in electrical and mechanical domains. While building an application, we often come across scenarios where we have to integrate with other applications/code, which are incompatible. Often, this results in lots of changes being made to either the base code or third-party code. But, in real-world scenarios, there can be various reasons wherein changes cannot be made to either the base code or third-party code or even both.

The **adapter design pattern** enables two incompatible classes to interact with each other, without those classes knowing about each other's implementation.

Universal Call Center is expanding and wants to enable its customers to pay via credit cards for their services. Assume that there is a third-party library available named `PaymentForYou`, which helps processing payments using PayPal. So, developers created a class that will send the payment processing request to a third-party library of `PaymentForYou`, which expects the request in XML format:

```
public class InvoicePaymentService{
  /**
  * This method invokes third party library to submit payment processing
  request
  */
  public void submitPaymentRequest(Invoice__c invoice){
  String xmlPaymentRequest;
  //... start
  //... some code to generate XML for payment processing
  //... finish
  //PaymentForYouProcessor is class name from third party
  // service with static method submitRequest
  PaymentForYouProcessor paymentProcessor = new PaymentForYouProcessor();
  paymentProcessor.submitRequest(xmlPaymentRequest);
  }
}
```

Further, similar code is implemented for various other requirements where payment processing is required, such as invoice payment, quote payment, recurring billing, and so on.

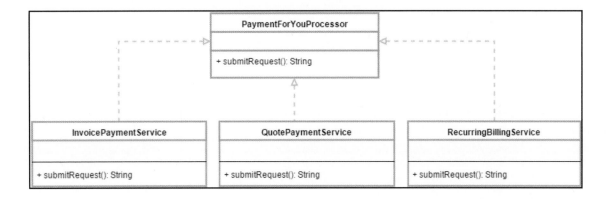

After six months, developers at Universal Call Center wanted to move to a different third-party payment processing service. As you can imagine, this means lots of changes to be made to the code wherever PaymentForYouProcessor is used in the existing code base. Further, all the changes will need rigorous testing and quality assurance checks.

So, the team decides to restructure the code to ensure that their functionalities are not tightly coupled with the payment service, and any changes made to the payment service can be managed/executed with ease and lesser impact.

The adapter pattern resolves the current problem by introducing the concept of the adapter class, which is responsible for working with two incompatible classes, to help them work together.

The following diagram shows how using a new PaymentAdapter adapter class, we can establish loose coupling between the PaymentForYouProcessor service and its implementation code:

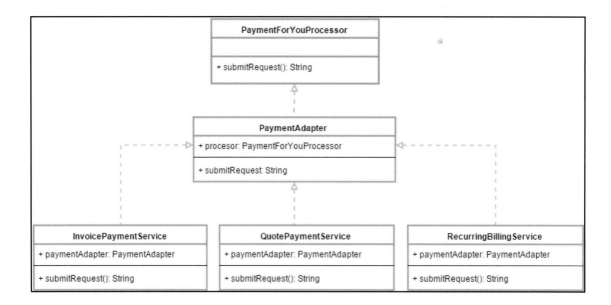

```
/**
 *    It interacts with external Payment service and loosely coupled
 *  with existing code
 * */
public class PaymentAdapter{
  PaymentForYouProcessor processor;
  //submit request to processor class to invoke payment processing
  public void submitRequest(String xmlData){
    processor.submitRequest(xmlData);
  }
}


public class InvoicePaymentService{
  /**
   * This method invokes third party library to submit payment processing
request
   */
  public void submitPaymentRequest(Invoice__c invoice){
    String xmlPaymentRequest;
    /**
     * code to generate XML for payment processing
     */
    PaymentAdapter adapter = new PaymentAdapter();
    adapter.submitRequest(xmlPaymentRequest);
  }
}

public class QuotePaymentService{
    /**
     * This method invokes third party library to submit payment processing
request
     */
  public void submitPaymentRequest(Quote invoice){
    String xmlPaymentRequest;
    /**
     * code to generate XML for payment processing
     */
    PaymentAdapter adapter = new PaymentAdapter();
    adapter.submitRequest(xmlPaymentRequest);
  }
}
```

As mentioned earlier, the `PaymentAdapter` adapter class creates an object of `PaymentForYouProcessor` and encapsulates the logic to invoke it. Hereby, all the underlying functionalities are not dependent on the `PaymentForYouProcessor` class directly. Any change in a third-party will mean a change in the adapter class only and not any other underlying classes. This is also known as the **object adapter pattern**.

The **object adapter pattern** encapsulates the third-party implementation and exposes the functionality in such a way that it is compatible with the application code. Hence, the application code is able to use the third-party code indirectly, without knowing the underlying implementation. It is important to note that the adapter class was identified at compile time while instantiating its class.

The object adapter pattern is very useful in situations where a service (generally, an external service) is to be used in multiple functionalities, and developers need to achieve loose coupling between a service and its implementations.

Some common scenarios are as follows:

- Integration with an external web service
- Using APIs provided by AppExchange applications

Now, with more and more customers using the online payment feature, users demand support for various other cards, such as MasterCard, American Express, and so on. Now, this poses another challenge for developers. With this sudden deluge of new payment processing types, developers want to achieve loose coupling between the application code and payment processing libraries. This approach will help teams to switch payment services at any time while having the least impact on the existing functionality. Assume that there is a third-party library named `PayByCard` that handles the payment using all major credit and debit cards available in the market.

However, `PayByCard` uses the JSON data format for data interchange as opposed to using XML. So, it becomes an additional complexity for all the application code to understand the data format that is expected by each payment library, that is, `PayByCard` (JSON) and `PaymentForYou` (XML).

The adapter pattern is also referred to as **glue code** as this code is generally used to patch up two distinct code sets.

Here, we can create an adapter implementation for each payment library. Further, each adapter will contain the logic to generate data in the required data format (XML or JSON) based on the underlying third-party payment library. This will help all the existing system functionalities to use any payment library uniformly and without changing any existing code.

We have already explored the factory method pattern in the previous chapter and know its advantage of being able to decouple code to instantiate objects. We can use this pattern to handle the instantiation of the correct adapter class to handle the payment processing.

The following table shows the various components used in our example:

Class category	Usage
Processor	These represent classes of a third-party library that cannot be changed. (`PaymentForYouProcessor` and `PayByCardProcessor`)
Adapter	These contain logic to interact with a processor class of a third-party library to provide uniform access (`PaymentForYouAdapter` and `PayByCardAdapter`)
Adapter contract	This contract needs to be implemented by all `PaymentAdapter` classes (`IPaymentAdapter`)
Wrapper	This works as a data carrier (`PaymetRequest`)
Factory	This helps instantiate an adapter at runtime (`PaymentAdapterFactory`)
Service	These are application code classes

The following class diagram shows the refactored code:

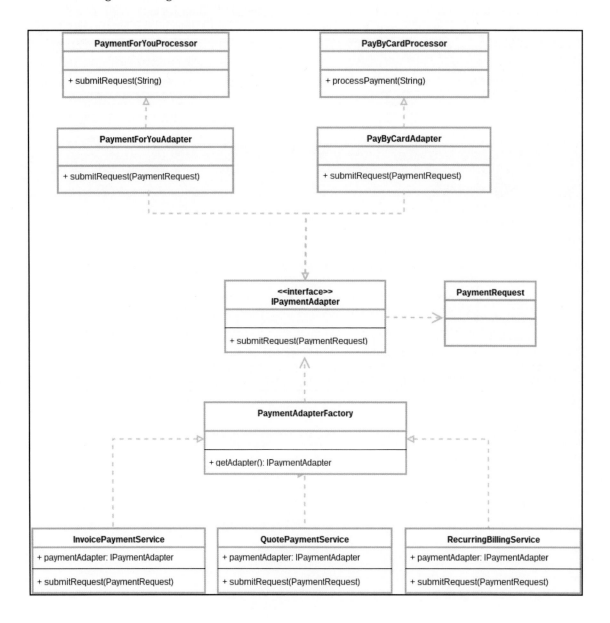

```java
/**
 * It interacts with external Payment service "PayByCard" and existing
 * code uses it via adapter resulting in loose coupling
 **/
public class PayByCardProcessor{
  public void processPayment(String jsonData){
    //process payment
  }
}

/**
 * It interacts with external Payment service "PaymentForYou" and
 * existing code uses it via adapter resulting in loose coupling
 **/
public class PaymentForYouProcessor{
  public void submitRequest(String xmlData){
    //Make API call to process payment
  }
}

/**
 * Data container class to be used to send data
 */
public class PaymentRequest{
  public Integer Amount {get; set;}
  public String PaymentMethod {get; set;}
  public String AuthorizationCode {get; set;}
}

/**
 * Factory for payment processor adapters
 */
public interface IPaymentAdapter{
  void submitRequest(PaymentRequest request);
}

/**
 * Adapter class for "PayByCard" payment service
 **/
public class PayByCardAdapter implements IPaymentAdapter{
  PayByCardProcessor processor;
  //submit request to processor class to invoke payment processing
  public void submitRequest(PaymentRequest request){
    String jSONData = generateJSONData(request);
    processor.processPayment(jSONData);
  }

  /*
```

```
     * placeholder method to generate JSON stream for payment
     * request as per underlying service requirements
     */
    String generateJSONData(PaymentRequest request){
      return 'JSON Data';
    }
  }


  /**
   * Adapter implementation for "PaymentForYou" payment service
   * Hides entire complexity to communicate to underlying service
   * */
  public class PaymentForYouAdapter implements IPaymentAdapter{
    PaymentForYouProcessor processor;
    //submit request to processor class to invoke payment processing
    public void submitRequest(PaymentRequest request){
      String xmlData = generateXMLData(request);
      processor.submitRequest(xmlData);
    }

    /*
     * placeholder method to generate XML stream for payment
     * request as per underlying service requirements
     */
    String generateXMLData(PaymentRequest request){
      return 'XML Data';
    }
  }


  /**
   * Factory class to generate Payment adapters
   **/
  public class PaymentAdapterFactory{

    public static IPaymentAdapter getAdapter(String adapterName){
      IPaymentAdapter adapter;
      if(adapterName == 'PaymentForYou'){
        adapter = new PaymentForYouAdapter();
      }
      else if(adapterName == 'PayByCard'){
        adapter = new PayByCardAdapter();
      }
      return adapter;
    }
  }

  /**
   * Implementation of quote payment functionality
```

```
  * */
public class QuotePaymentService{
  /**
    * This method invokes third party library to submit
    * payment processing request
    */
  public void submitPaymentRequest(Quote invoice){
    PaymentRequest quotePaymentRequest;
    //send payment processing request
    IPaymentAdapter adapter = PaymentAdapterFactory.getAdapter('PayNow');
    adapter.submitRequest(quotePaymentRequest);
  }
}


/**
  * Implementation of invoice payment functionality
  * */
public class InvoicePaymentService{
  /**
    * This method invokes third party library to submit
    * payment processing request
    */
  public void submitPaymentRequest(Invoice__c invoice){
    PaymentRequest invoicePaymentRequest;
    //send payment processing request
    IPaymentAdapter adapter =
PaymentAdapterFactory.getAdapter('PaymentForYou');
    adapter.submitRequest(invoicePaymentRequest);
  }
}
```

As shown in the preceding code, all the application service classes
(`QuotePaymentService` and `InvoicePaymentService`) use adapter's
submitRequest method. It further invokes the payment processing mechanism for all payment
processors uniformly, irrespective of the method name for each third-party payment
processors (`PaymentForyourProcessor` and `PayByCardProcessor`).

Additionally, the underlying complexity to send data in the expected data format
(JSON/XML), as required by each payment processor class, is also hidden from the
application classes.

The preceding approach is the runtime implementation of adapters, wherein the application
class doesn't know which adapter to use at compile time, also known as the **runtime
adapter pattern**. This is an excellent example of blending two design patterns (factory
method and adapter patterns) and creating an innovative solution.

The **runtime adapter pattern** helps incompatible classes to interact with each other dynamically.

Points to consider

- The adapter pattern helps solve incompatibility issues between the existing code.

- Both the faÃ§ade and adapter design patterns use the wrapper class. However, the adapter pattern is used to allow interactions between the existing systems, but the faÃ§ade pattern is used to create a new simplified interface.

- The object adapter pattern is recommended to be used where there is only one type of third-party library involved.

- The runtime adapter pattern is recommended to be used where you need to support multiple third-party libraries.

The bridge pattern

There can be situations where multiple modules of an application are being built together and changed frequently. Due to high dependency, the probability of breaking the code is prominent.

To understand this pattern, we first need to understand the problem. Assume that a web development company wants to build and launch a new web framework. To speed up the development cycle, they decide to create two teams: the *Core framework* and *User experience (UX)* team. As the name suggests the Core framework team will be responsible for designing and implementing the core of the framework and the UX team will be responsible for the user interface. Initially, it was decided that the framework will support two types of websites: **Blog** and **Content Management System (CMS)**. In the same way, they decided to release two themes named **White Blue** and **White Green**.

The team came up with the following class structure at a high level:

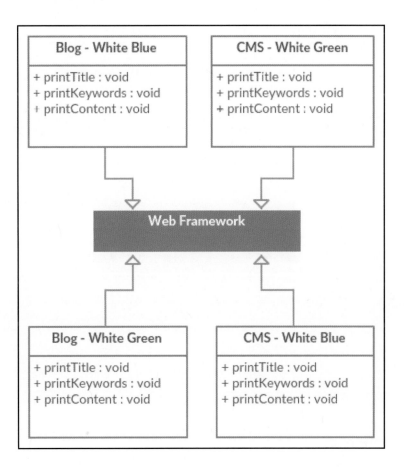

After taking a look at this class diagram, the team understood that this is not going to work. Let's say that if we need to add one more website type such as **News**, then the code structure will look like the following figure:

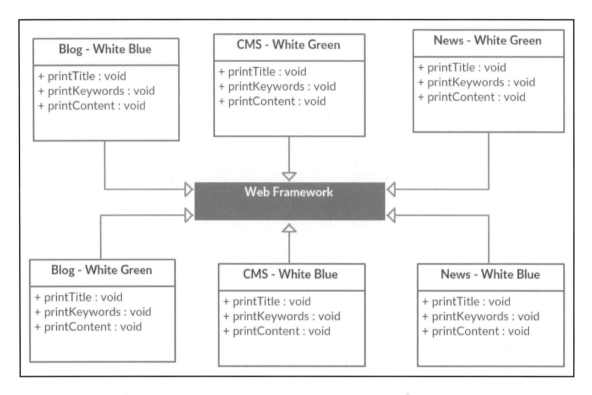

If the Core framework supported is denoted by "a" and the supported Theme is denoted by "b", then in this case, the total "a x b" number of classes needs to be created.

Both the modules, the Core framework and UX, are undergoing frequent changes and hence cannot be dependent on each other. We need some kind of a mechanism where they should be able to communicate, and at the same time, allow changes without impacting each other. In other words, we need a *bridge* to allow the communication between the Core framework and Theme modules.

The **bridge pattern** decouples an abstraction from its implementation so that both can be changed independently.

We will start with the Theme first. All the themes should be able to apply styles to the header, footer, menu, and content. We can say that every theme should provide these features, and we can enforce them with the help of an interface:

```
public interface ITheme{
  void styleHeader();
  void styleFooter();
  void styleMenu();
  void styleContent();
}
```

All the Theme classes will implement the preceding interface. In our case, we have two themes: WhiteBlue and WhiteGreen:

```
public class Theme_WhiteBlue implements ITheme{
  public void styleHeader(){
    System.debug('Header - Font size : 16px, '+
      'Background : Blue, Color : Black');
  }
  public void styleFooter(){
    System.debug('Footer - Font size : 14px, '+
      'Background : White, Color : Blue');
  }
  public void styleMenu(){
    System.debug('Menu - Font size : 12px, '+
      'Background : Blue, Color : White');
  }

  public void styleContent(){
    System.debug('Content - Font size : 16px, '+
     'Background : White, Color : Black');
  }
}
```

In the same way, we will create the other theme class, Theme_WhiteGreen, on the basis of an ITheme interface:

```
public class Theme_WhiteGreen implements ITheme{
  public void styleHeader(){
    System.debug('Header - Font size : 16px, '+
      'Background : Green, Color : Black');
  }

  public void styleFooter(){
    System.debug('Footer - Font size : 14px, '+
      'Background : White, Color : Green');
  }
```

```
   public void styleMenu(){
     System.debug('Menu - Font size : 12px, '+
       'Background : Green, Color : White');
   }

   public void styleContent(){
     System.debug('Content - Font size : 16px, '+
       'Background : White, Color : Black');
   }
}
```

To create the WebFramework class, we need to know some basic operations that almost all website types should support, such as displaying the title, keywords (metatag), and page content. In the same way, features such as a header, footer, and menu are supported by all website types. However, if they need to be changed, then the framework should be able to support it. The abstract class is the most suitable in our example as it allows us to define a default behavior, which can also be overridden as per our requirements:

```
public abstract class WebFramework{
  protected ITheme theme;
  private String title;
  private String keyword;
  private String content;
  //Child class must implement it
  public abstract void capability();
  public void setProperties(String title, String keyword,
                            String content){
    this.title = title;
    this.keyword = keyword;
    this.content = content;
  }

  public void printTitle(){
    System.debug('Title - '+title);
  }

  public void printKeyword(){
    System.debug('Keyword - '+keyword);
  }

  public void printContent(){
    System.debug('Content - '+content);
  }

  //constructor

  public WebFramework(ITheme t){
```

```
    theme = t;
  }

  //Child class can reuse this method or override it

  public virtual void showHeader_Footer(){
    theme.styleHeader();
    theme.styleFooter();
  }

  //Child class can reuse this method or override it

  public virtual void showMenu_Body(){
    theme.styleMenu();
    theme.styleContent();
  }
}
```

The first website type that can be based on the Core framework is **Blog**, as shown in the following code:

```
public class BlogFramework extends WebFramework{
  public BlogFramework(ITheme t){
    //Call constructor of parent class
    super(t);
  }

  public override void capability(){
    System.debug('This is Blog Framework and does not support Menu');
  }

  //As blog does not support Menu, we will not style it

  public override void showMenu_Body(){
    theme.styleContent();
  }
}
```

The preceding blog framework does not support the menu and, therefore, we changed its implementation in a child class.

 The super method can be used to call a constructor of a parent class in Apex.

```
public class CMSFramework extends WebFramework{
  public CMSFramework(ITheme t){
    //Call constructor of parent class
    super(t);
  }

  public override void capability(){
    System.debug('This is CMS Framework and supports workflow to publish
public content');
  }
}
```

In the case of CMS, only the capability needs to be implemented. The other functionality is used directly from the abstract class.

The following anonymous code shows the bridge pattern in action.

Code snippet one is as follows:

```
WebFramework webFrameowrk = new BlogFramework(new Theme_WhiteBlue());
webFrameowrk.setProperties('Salesforce Blog', 'Salesforce, Design
Pattern','Article on Bridge Pattern');
webFrameowrk.printKeyword();
webFrameowrk.printTitle();
webFrameowrk.printContent();
webFrameowrk.showHeader_Footer();
webFrameowrk.showMenu_Body();
```

The output is as follows:

```
Keyword - Salesforce, Design Pattern
Title - Salesforce Blog
Content - Article on Bridge Pattern
Header - Font size : 16px, Background : Blue, Color : Black
Footer - Font size : 14px, Background : White, Color : Blue
Content - Font size : 16px, Background : White, Color : Black
```

Code snippet two is as follows:

```
WebFramework webFrameowrk = new CMSFramework(new Theme_WhiteGreen());
webFrameowrk.setProperties('Salesforce Community CMS', 'Non Profit
Information','First Post on NPSP');
webFrameowrk.printKeyword();
webFrameowrk.printTitle();
webFrameowrk.printContent();
webFrameowrk.showHeader_Footer();
webFrameowrk.showMenu_Body();
```

The output is as follows:

```
Keyword - Non Profit Information
Title - Salesforce Community CMS
Content - First Post on NPSP
Header - Font size : 16px, Background : Green, Color : Black
Footer - Font size : 14px, Background : White, Color : Green
Menu - Font size : 12px, Background : Green, Color : White
Content - Font size : 16px, Background : White, Color : Black
```

The following figure shows the class diagram of the example that we discussed:

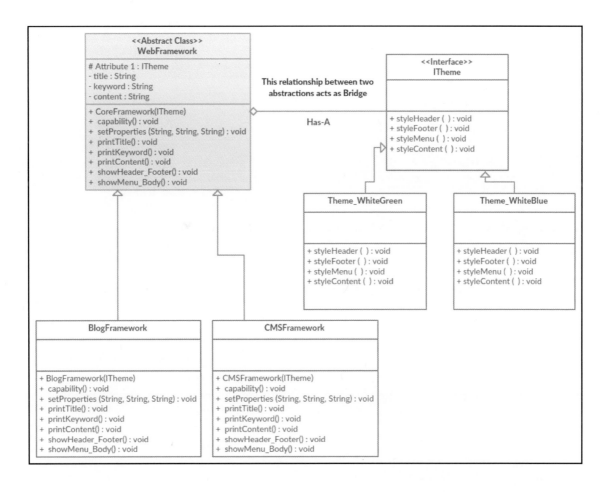

The preceding example shows that the Core framework and UX are completely independent and can be changed simultaneously without impacting each other. Both the modules communicate with each other and show the power of abstraction in OOP. In future, if a new website type gets added, there will be no impact on the Theme and vice versa.

The following figure summarizes the before and after implementation of a system using the bridge pattern:

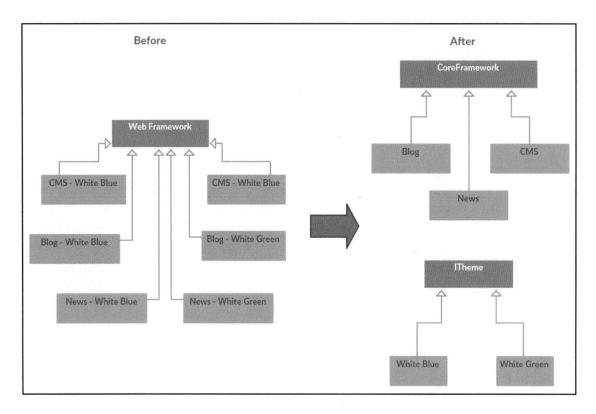

Has-a relationship (composition) is used to create a *bridge* between `WebFramework` and `Theme` classes.

Has-a relationship

Has-a relationship in OOPs normally denotes a composition. An instance of one class is used in another class. For example, Honda has an engine. In this example, Honda is an object and engine is a different object, but the engine object is referred in the Honda class.

Points to consider

- The bridge pattern supports the usage of a composition. In the preceding example as well, the Core framework class consists of a reference to the theme class.
- The adapter pattern works for the existing code; however, in the bridge pattern, we design it from the beginning.
- The bridge pattern is often confused with the strategy pattern. However, the strategy pattern is meant for runtime polymorphism. The bridge pattern is a structural pattern where the code changes frequently and its implementation is decoupled from its abstraction.

The composite pattern

Universal Call Center recently started providing customer support for online retail businesses. It is required to track details of products shipped in any order consignment. One order can have multiple products. Developers came up with the following simple Apex class:

```
public class Product{
    public String universalProductCode { get; set; }
    public Decimal cost { get; set; }
}
```

The preceding class stores the required information about one product. One order can have multiple products, so we need one more class to represent an order, as shown in the following code:

```
public class Order{
    public List<Product > lstProducts {get; set; }
    /**
     * Total products one Order
     * */
    public integer totalProducts() {
        if(lstProducts != null)
            return lstProducts.size();
        return 0;
    }
    /**
     * Total cost of Order
     * */
    public Decimal totalCost(){
```

```
            Decimal cost = 0;
            if(lstProducts != null){
                for(Product p : lstProducts){
                    cost = cost+p.cost ;
                }
            }
            return cost;
        }
    }
```

We can use the following code from the anonymous Apex window to test the code:

```
List<Product> lstProducts = new List<Product>();

Product  item = new Product();
item.universalProductCode = '123456789999' ;
item.cost = 200;
lstProducts.add(item);

Product  item1 = new Product();
item1.universalProductCode = '123456745999' ;
item1.cost = 550;
lstProducts.add(item1);

Order order = new Order();
order.lstProducts = lstProducts ;

System.debug('Total Products - '+order.totalProducts());
System.debug('Total Cost - '+order.totalCost());
```

The output is as follows:

```
Total Products - 2
Total Cost - 750
```

So far, the coding approach seems to be adequate, until a new requirement was shared. Online retailer clients of Universal Call Center identified that each order was being shipped separately, leading to rising shipping charges. They realized that if orders addressed to the same area can be shipped together, it will result in significant cost savings.

Hence, the concept of a **pantry** was introduced. A pantry can be considered a shipment of shipments. A pantry can contain a product or another pantry. So, with this structure, a single shipment can club together multiple shipments from the same area. Hereby, providing cost savings. The following diagram shows the same idea that we discussed:

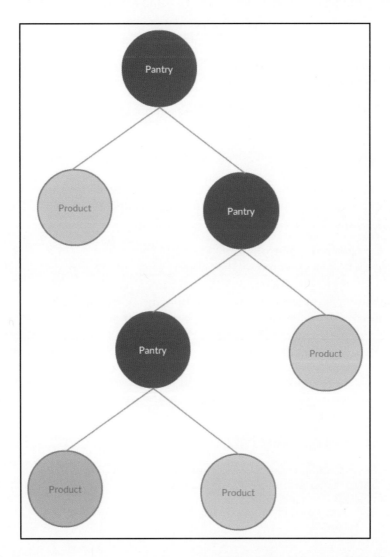

In the preceding diagram, a leaf node represents a **Product** and a non-leaf node represents a **Pantry**.

Developers realized that they need to support the hierarchy of objects to be able to support the preceding structure, as shown in the preceding diagram. To achieve modularity, it is very important to ensure that the product and pantry can be handled the same way in an application. For example, when an application needs to calculate the total number of items or total cost, the product and pantry should both be able to support the same operation.

In the case of a product, an application will need information about that product only. However, in the case of a pantry, the application will need information about all the enclosed products and pantries. Also, a pantry will need some additional methods to add or remove items from another pantry.

The **composite design pattern** helps interact uniformly with a part as well as part-whole hierarchy.

In the composite design pattern, an object is composed of a tree structure, where a leaf node represents an item and a composite node represents a collection of items. This is used to represent a part-whole relationship.

A part-whole relationship
In OOP, a part-whole relationship is a specific type of relationship where an object has its own life cycle and can be part of the other object. For example, you can consider a relationship between teachers and departments. One teacher (part) can be part of many departments (whole). If a department is deleted, a teacher still exists and can remain part of the other departments.

We need to make sure that both the product and pantry have a uniform behavior. We cannot use an interface in our code because the pantry will have some extra methods, so we will use the `abstract class`:

```
public abstract class Item{
  // Custom Exception class to throw an error
  public class UnSupportedOperationException extends Exception{}
  //By default items will be '1' in count
  public virtual integer getTotalItems(){
    return 1;
  }
  //Child class can either implement this or leave this unimplemented
  public virtual void addItem(Item i) {
    throw new UnSupportedOperationException('AddItem() method is not
supported');
  }
  //Child class can either implement this or leave this unimplemented
```

```
  public virtual void removeItem(Integer index) {
    throw new UnSupportedOperationException('removeItem() method is not
supported');
  }
  //Child class can either implement this or leave this unimplemented
  public virtual Item getItem(Integer index){
    throw new UnSupportedOperationException('getItem() method is not
supported');
  }

  //This method is only needed in Product class not in Pantry
  public virtual String getUPC(){
    throw new UnSupportedOperationException('getUPC() method is not
supported');
  }
  //All child class must implement this abstract class
  public abstract Double getCost();
}
```

 We cannot instantiate the standard `Exception` class in Apex. As we need
to throw an exception, the custom exception class needs to be created by
extending the `Exception` class.

As shown in the preceding class, some methods throw a custom exception,
`UnSupportedOperationException`, as these methods may or may not apply to child
classes.

Let's see how we can write a `Pantry` class:

```
public class Pantry extends Item{
  private List<Item> lstItems;
  //Constructor
  public Pantry(){
    lstItems = new List<Item>() ;
  }
  public override Integer getTotalItems(){
    return lstItems.size();
  }
  public override void addItem(Item i){
    lstItems.add(i);
  }
  public override void removeItem(Integer index){
    if(lstItems.size() >= index)
      lstItems.remove(index);
  }
  public override Item getItem(Integer index)
```

```
  {
    if(lstItems.size() >= index)
      return lstItems[index];
      return null;
  }
  //Get cost from each product inside pantry
  public override Double getCost(){
    Double totalCost = 0;
    for(Item i : lstItems){
      totalCost = totalCost + i.getCost();
    }
    return totalCost;
  }
}
```

As we can see in the preceding `Pantry` class, we have implemented all the possible operations supported by a pantry.

Let's refactor our `Product` class to implement the composite design pattern:

```
public class Product extends Item{
  private String universalProductCode ;
  private Double cost;

  //constructor
  public Product(String upc, Integer price){
    universalProductCode = upc;
    cost = price;
  }
  public override Double getCost(){
    return cost;
  }
  public override String getUPC(){
    return universalProductCode;
  }
}
```

As you may have noticed, only the `getCost` and `getUPC` methods have been overridden. The remaining methods, such as `addItem` and `removeItem` are not overridden as they are not applicable to products.

To demonstrate the magic of the *composite pattern*, we have recreated the `Order` class, as shown in the following code:

```
public class Order {
  private List<Item> lstItems ;
  public void loadShipmentsItems(List<Item> lstI){
```

```
      lstItems = lstI;
   }
   // The following method shows advantage of composite pattern
   public Double getTotalValueOfOrder(){
     DOuble totalVal = 0;
     for(Item i : lstItems){
       // method getCost() is used uniformly
       totalVal = totalVal + i.getCost();
     }
     return totalVal ;
   }
   public Integer getTotalItems(){
     Integer totalItems = 0;
     for(Item i : lstItems){
       // method getTotalItems () is used uniformly
       totalItems = totalItems + i.getTotalItems();
     }
     return totalItems;
   }
}
```

In the preceding code, even if `Order` has multiple products or a combination of products and pantries, it interacts with both the type of objects uniformly to get the total cost and total number of products in order. The advantages of using the composite pattern can be seen very clearly here.

Let's test and see how the code works from the anonymous Apex by running the following code snippet:

```
List<Item> lstItems = new List<Item>();

//Two products to be part of pantry "p"
Product amazonEcho = new Product('89065437074',178) ;
Product iphone6s = new Product('5680863467',200);

//The following pantry will become part of other pantry
Pantry pantryInsidePantry = new Pantry();
pantryInsidePantry.addItem(new Product('5654465318' , 10));
pantryInsidePantry.addItem(new Product('5654465788' , 10));

//The following pantry contains products and pantries
Pantry p = new Pantry();
p.addItem(new Product('5678953188' , 890));
p.addItem(new Product('5645654318' , 100));
p.addItem(new Product('5898595318' , 20));
p.addItem(new Product('5656744318' , 89));
p.addItem(pantryInsidePantry);
```

```
lstItems.add(amazonEcho);
lstItems.add(iphone6s);
lstItems.add(p);

Order o = new Order();
o.loadShipmentsItems(lstItems);
System.debug('Total Items in Shipment '+o.getTotalItems());
System.debug('Total value of Shipment '+o.getTotalValueOfOrder());
```

The output of the preceding code snippet is as follows:

```
Total Items in Shipment 7
Total value of Shipment 1497.0
```

The following class diagram shows the complete implementation of the composite design pattern:

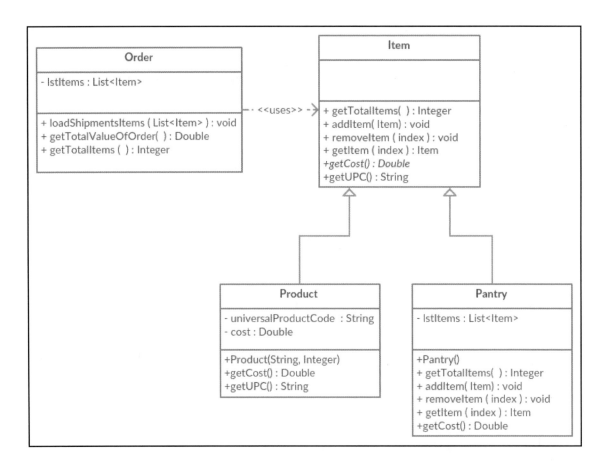

As discussed earlier, the composite pattern shows that it makes the code modular and efficient by treating different types of objects uniformly. This is also one of the examples that demonstrate the Liskov substitution principal (**L** in the SOLID principal), as discussed in `Chapter 1`, *An Introduction to Apex Design Pattern*, where objects in an application should be replaced by instances of their child implementations without altering the correctness of a program.

Other use cases

Let's take another example; we want to evaluate a logical expression, which is a combination of OR and AND operators. For example, an expression can be as follows:

(A AND (B OR C)) AND D

In the preceding expression, we can consider D as the leaf node (similar to **Product**) and the AND and OR operators as composite nodes (similar to **Pantry**).

Points to consider

- The composite design pattern uses a recursion to traverse the entire hierarchy. In our case, pantry is a nonleaf node and we iterate it until we find products inside a pantry.
- This design pattern is mostly used in one-to-many relationships. In our case, one pantry can consist of multiple pantries or products.
- We have used polymorphism using inheritance where we used both pantry and product interchangeably because they share the same parent class.

The decorator pattern

Universal Call Center is planning to support technical issues of end customers. These call center agents are basically going to work on two types of issues, which may be related to point and click or development. However, not necessarily every customer issue will be resolved with only the point and click or development solution. It might be possible that a customer wants to resolve the data loader issue as well, in addition to an admin issue (point and click). A few customers may want integration issues to be resolved, some other customers may ask for Apex issues to be fixed, and so on. Salesforce is such a big product that the requirements of all the customers will not fit into two simple plans.

The following diagram shows an attempt made by developers to solve this problem using inheritance:

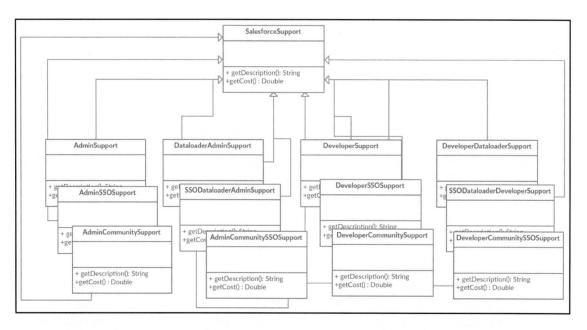

From the preceding diagram, we can understand that there are lots of classes with repetitive code. There can be numerous other combinations of the support model, which will result in more similar classes.

So, inheritance is clearly not a good choice in this scenario. Developers decided to use object composition (do not confuse it with the composite pattern). The composition approach will surely be advantageous in this case. Developers will use an object of the existing class and add more properties as needed, without changing the original class. Anything that they want to add will be in a new class, which will act as a decorator.

> The **decorator design pattern** adds an additional functionality to the existing objects at runtime to achieve a single objective. This pattern explain a scenario where the composition of objects can be more beneficial than inheritance.

The following abstract class needs to be inherited by all the core support model classes (for example, Apex, and admin support models):

```
public abstract class SalesforceSupport{
  //give description of support
  public virtual String getDescription(){
    return 'This is base Abstract class';
  }
  /**
   * This methods must be implemented by all child classes.
   * It returns total cost to resolve case of specific type.
   * */
  public abstract Double getCost();
}
```

As discussed, there can be two types of support classes. The following two classes show how the admin and Apex support classes can be implemented.

The following code assumes that the admin support ticket costs 25 USD per issue to a client:

```
public class AdminSupport extends SalesforceSupport{
  Integer totalCase = 1 ;
  public AdminSupport( Integer totalCasePerMonth)
  {
    totalCase = totalCasePerMonth;
  }
  /**
   * Total cost to resolve one case
   * */
  public override Double getCost(){
    return 25.0 * totalCase ;
  }
  public override String getDescription(){
    return 'This class represents informations related to Admin cases';
  }
}
```

It is assumed that Apex support costs 80 USD per ticket:

```
public class ApexSupport extends SalesforceSupport{
  Integer totalCase = 1 ;
  public ApexSupport( Integer totalCasePerMonth)
  {
    totalCase = totalCasePerMonth;
  }
  /**
   * Total cost to resolve one case
```

```
   * */
  public override Double getCost(){
    return 80.0* totalCase ;
  }
  public override String getDescription(){
    return 'This class represents informations related to Apex and Trigger
classes';
  }
}
```

In addition to Apex or admin support, a customer can ask for help in resolving issues related to the data loader, community, SSO, and so on. This is similar to a pizza where a pizza is the actual product (in our case, Apex and admin support) and a customer can ask for any combination of toppings (in our case, data loader, community, or SSO).

All the additional support types can be added to the core support type with the help of decorator classes. The following code declares a decorator abstract class, which extends SalesforceSupport, so that properties can be added to the existing support types without altering the original form:

```
public abstract class SalesforceSupportDecorator extends SalesforceSupport{
  public abstract override String getDescription() ;
}
```

The following class represents the data loader request, which costs an additional 80 USD per issue:

```
public class DataLoaderSupport extends SalesforceSupportDecorator{
  SalesforceSupport support ;
  Integer totalCase = 1 ;
  public DataLoaderSupport(SalesforceSupport s, Integer totalCasePerMonth)
  {
    support = s;
    totalCase = totalCasePerMonth;
  }
  /**
   * Override getCost of parent of parent
   * */
  public override Double getCost(){
    return 80.0 * totalCase + support.getCost();
  }
  public override String getDescription(){
    return support.getDescription() + ', Decorator class -
DataLoaderSupport';
  }
}
```

The following class is a decorator class of the community support, which costs 35 USD per ticket:

```
public class CommunitySupport extends SalesforceSupportDecorator{
  SalesforceSupport support ;
  Integer totalCase = 1 ;
  public CommunitySupport(SalesforceSupport s, Integer totalCasePerMonth)
  {
    support = s;
    totalCase = totalCasePerMonth;
  }
  /**
   * Total cost to resolve one case
   * */
  public override Double getCost(){
    return 35.0 * totalCase + support.getCost();
  }
  public override String getDescription(){
    return support.getDescription() + ', Decorator class -
CommunitySupport';
  }
}
```

The following Apex class is a decorator class for the SSO support that costs 65 USD to a customer:

```
public class SSOSupport extends SalesforceSupportDecorator {
  SalesforceSupport support ;
  Integer totalCase = 1 ;
  public SSOSupport(SalesforceSupport s, Integer totalCasePerMonth)
  {
    support = s;
    totalCase = totalCasePerMonth;
  }
  /**
   * Total cost to resolve one case
   * */
  public override Double getCost(){
    return 65.0  * totalCase + support.getCost();
  }
  public override String getDescription(){
    return support.getDescription() + ', Decorator class -
CommunitySupport';
  }
}
```

To get more idea of how it works, let's create the following sample class:

```
public class DecoratorPatternSupport{
  /**
   * This method computes total cost for month for Dataloader,
   * Community and Admin Cases
   * */
  public static void getDataloaderCommunityAdminCost(Integer
adminCaseCount, Integer communityCaseCount, Integer dataloaderCaseCount){
     SalesforceSupport admin = new AdminSupport(adminCaseCount);
     admin = new CommunitySupport(admin, communityCaseCount);
     admin = new DataLoaderSupport(admin, dataloaderCaseCount);
     System.debug(' Total Cost of all Supports - '+admin.getCost());
     System.debug(' Description of all support cases types-
'+admin.getDescription());
  }
  /**
   * This method computes total cost for month for Dataloader,
   * Community and Admin Cases
   * */
  public static void getSSODeveloperCost(Integer developerCaseCount,
Integer ssoCaseCount ){
     SalesforceSupport dev = new ApexSupport(developerCaseCount);
     dev = new SSOSupport(dev, ssoCaseCount);
     System.debug(' Total Cost of all Supports - '+dev.getCost());
     System.debug(' Description of all support cases types-
'+dev.getDescription());
  }
}
```

In the preceding source code, we first created an instance of the admin support. Now, this admin support is considered the original object, and in order to change its behavior, we will need to add some decorators, such as community and data loader. These decorators will not alter any existing property of admin support, but they will add an additional functionality.

The following figure shows how decorator objects calculate the cost of admin support, community support, and data loader support by interacting with enclosed entities:

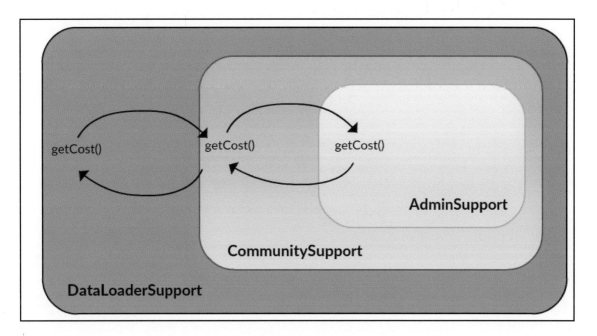

Run the following code snippet on the developer console:

```
//Get cost of 50 Admin, 1 Data loader and 1 Community support ticket
DecoratorPatternSupport.getDataloaderCommunityAdminCost(50,1,1);

//Get cost of 50 developer and 10 SSO request
DecoratorPatternSupport.getSSODeveloperCost(50,10);
```

We will get the following output:

```
Total Cost of all Supports - 1365.0
Description of all support cases types- This class represents informations
related to Admin cases, Decorator class - CommunitySupport, Decorator class
- DataLoaderSupport

Total Cost of all Supports - 4650.0
 Description of all support cases types- This class represents informations
related to Apex and Trigger classes, Decorator class - CommunitySupport
```

The following figure shows the final class diagram:

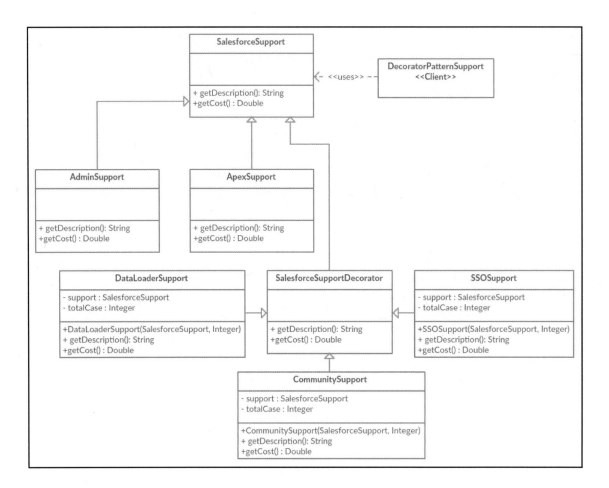

Other use cases

The Salesforce official blog has one good example of the decorator pattern. It shows that if some calculation is needed on the fly for the Visualforce page, then the wrapper class can be used for preprocessing or on the fly calculation. In this way, we do not need to create a temporary formula field, and therefore, there is no change in the existing SObject schema. This post can be found at

https://developer.salesforce.com/page/Apex_Design_Patterns_-_Decorator_ sObject.

Points to consider

- Most people get confused with the composite and decorator patterns. The composite design pattern provides *uniform* access to the part or part-whole hierarchy, whereas the decorator pattern can add a new behavior without changing its enclosed entity.

- The adapter pattern wraps an object and changes its interface to make it compatible with the client application. The decorator pattern adds more features to a wrapped object but doesn't change its interface.

The flyweight pattern

It is always recommended that you design code with a memory-efficient approach to ensure that the memory footprint of the code is lean, and hence, less likely to clog the system. In the case of the Salesforce platform, it is extremely important as Salesforce imposes various limits, such as governor limits, feature limits, and so on. So, it is advisable to keep track of resource consumption.

The flyweight pattern was initially coined and used by Paul Calder and Mark Linton in relation to the **What-You-See-Is-What-You-Get (WYSIWYG)** visual editor development. As **Graphical User Interface (GUI)** applications are memory intensive, the flyweight pattern was used to handle memory efficiently.

The flyweight pattern helps reduce the memory footprint of the code and hence is very beneficial in Apex/Visualforce programming. It can help developers reduce the usage of heap memory and viewstate, in turn, avoiding governor limit-related violations. Furthermore, lesser viewstate also means an improved page performance.

 Visualforce enables developers to create forms, which can help pass data back and forth between the client browser and server based on the user's actions. Each time a page is loaded (initial load or subsequent postback), its controller (Apex) state is automatically reinstated. Visualforce handles it automatically by serializing the state of a controller and passing it to the client. This serialized state is called **viewstate**. Viewstate contains all the data attributes of a controller, objects that are directly or indirectly accessible by the controller's properties, and other details required by Visualforce.

Continuing with our journey, Universal Call Center is implementing a products list screen, which displays a list of products with their information:

Name	Product Code	Tax Rate	Tax Type	Total Tax	Vendor Name	Shipping Address	Vendor Phone	Vendor Email
GenWatt Diesel 200kW	GC1040	1.5	Entertainment Tax	$ 300.00	XYZ Corp	A-34 Oakwood ave., Santa Clara	345-435-2345	sales@abccopr.com
GenWatt Diesel 10kW	GC1020	0.5	Luxury Tax	$ 150.00	ABC Corp	123 Park street, Mount View	345-435-2345	sales@abccopr.com
Installation: Industrial - High	IN7080	2	Service Tax	$ 200.00	ABC Corp	123 Park street, Mount View	345-435-2345	sales@abccopr.com
SLA: Silver	SL9040	1.5	Entertainment Tax	$ 300.00	XYZ Corp	A-34 Oakwood ave., Santa Clara	345-435-2345	sales@abccopr.com
GenWatt Propane 500kW	GC3040	0.5	Luxury Tax	$ 150.00	ABC Corp	123 Park street, Mount View	345-435-2345	sales@abccopr.com
SLA: Platinum	SL9080	2	Service Tax	$ 200.00	ABC Corp	123 Park street, Mount View	345-435-2345	sales@abccopr.com
GenWatt Propane 100kW	GC3020	1.5	Entertainment Tax	$ 300.00	XYZ Corp	A-34 Oakwood ave., Santa Clara	345-435-2345	sales@abccopr.com
GenWatt Propane 1500kW	GC3060	0.5	Luxury Tax	$ 150.00	ABC Corp	123 Park street, Mount View	345-435-2345	sales@abccopr.com
GenWatt Diesel 1000kW	GC1060	2	Service Tax	$ 200.00	ABC Corp	123 Park street, Mount View	345-435-2345	sales@abccopr.com
SLA: Bronze	SL9020	1.5	Entertainment Tax	$ 300.00	XYZ Corp	A-34 Oakwood ave., Santa Clara	345-435-2345	sales@abccopr.com

Developers design a wrapper class to display the information, as shown in the following figure:

```
+-------------------------------------+
|           ProductWrapper            |
+-------------------------------------+
|                                     |
+-------------------------------------+
| String Name                         |
| String ProductCode                  |
| Decimal SalesPrice                  |
| Decimal TaxRate                     |
| String TaxType                      |
| String TaxDetails                   |
| Decimal TotalTax                    |
| String VendorName                   |
| String VendorShippingAddress        |
| String VendorContactPhone           |
| String VendorContactEmail           |
+-------------------------------------+
```

```
public class ProductWrapper{

    //public properties
    public String Name {get; set;}
    public String ProductCode {get; set;}
    public Decimal SalesPrice {get; set;}
    public Decimal TaxRate {get; set;}
    public String TaxType {get; set;}
    public String TaxDetails {get; set;}
    public Decimal TotalTax {get; set;}
    public String VendorName {get; set;}
    public String VendorShippingAddress {get; set;}
    public String VendorContactPhone {get; set;}
    public String VendorContactEmail {get; set;}
    //constructor
    public ProductWrapper(String name, String productCode){
      this.Name = name;
      this.ProductCode = productCode;
    }
  }
}
```

In the preceding wrapper class, each instance of `ProductWrapper` contains product, tax, and vendor details. As the product list grows, the overall viewstate of the page also increases. The development team identifies that with this behavior, a page can easily hit viewstate limits (135 KB) and can result in an unstable functionality.

> A **wrapper class** in Apex is a class that contains another object or a list of objects. This class normally acts as a container class and is used mostly to perform some additional logic, which is not supported by the original enclosed object.

The team tries to identify various options to minimize the page's viewstate. In Apex, the first and the most obvious suggestion in such scenarios is to mark memory-intensive properties as *transient*.

The **transient** keyword is used in Apex to denote a controller's property, which should not be saved in viewstate. This means that the state (values) of transient properties are not persisted between the page's postback sessions.

Nontransient properties are persisted and sent back and forth during page postbacks. Hence, we are able to recover the previous state (values) of any properties automatically.

We cannot use the transient variable in this case because if we use it, the state (properties) of products between Visualforce and the Apex controller will be lost. Also, in order to retrieve an applicable tax bracket for a product, a lot of processing is required, which will need to be repeated again on each postback, leading to degraded performance.

Transient versus static

Transient should not be confused with static. Static variables are maintained and shared at class level, wherein transient is stored at object level. Both static and transient properties are destructed when a page is loaded or unloaded.

Again, a technical architect jumps for help and suggests that the team should consider the flyweight design pattern.

The **flyweight design pattern** identifies common or repetitive data within an object and then makes it reusable by storing it at a shared location.

So in the previous scenario, the technical architect suggests creating separate wrapper classes for tax brackets and the vendor. Instances of these wrapper classes can be used in the `Product` class. This way, the actual instance count of tax brackets can be minimized and can be reused between all products. Hence, it greatly reduces the viewstate size of the page.

The following diagram shows the final class structure after implementing the flyweight design pattern:

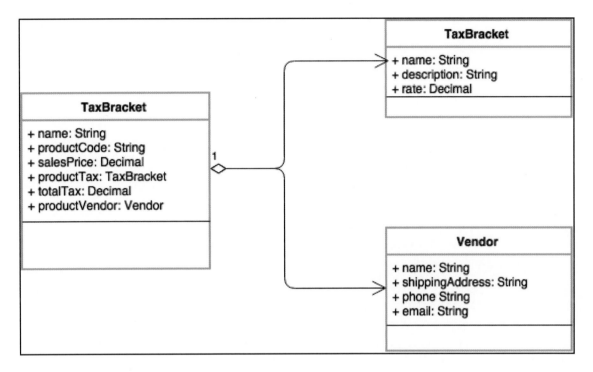

The following code represents the tax bracket and vendor flyweight classes:

```
//Tax Bracket Flyweight class
public class TaxBracket{
  public String Name {get; set;}
  public String Description {get; set;}
  public Decimal Rate {get; set;}
  public TaxBracket(String name, String description, Decimal rate){
    this.Name = name;
    this.Description = description;
    this.Rate = rate;
  }
}

//Vendor Flyweight class
public class Vendor{
  public String Name {get; set;}
  public String ShippingAddress {get; set;}
  public String Phone {get; set;}
```

```
  public String Email {get; set;}
  public Vendor(String name, String address, String phone,
  String email){
    this.Name = name;
    this.ShippingAddress = address;
    this.phone = phone;
    this.Email = email;
  }
}
```

Now, the product class can be refactored as follows:

```
public class ProductWrapper{
    public String Name {get; set;}
    public String ProductCode {get; set;}
    public Decimal SalesPrice {get; set;}
    public Attachment ProductAttachment {get; set;}
    public Decimal TotalTax {get; set;}
    public Vendor ProductVendor {get; set;}
    public TaxBracket ProductTax {get; set;}
    public ProductWrapper(String name, String productCode,
        Decimal salesPrice, Vendor productVendor,
        TaxBracket productTax){
        this.Name = name;
        this.ProductCode = productCode;
        this.ProductVendor = productVendor;
        this.ProductTax = productTax;
        this.SalesPrice = salesPrice;
        this.TotalTax = (salesPrice * productTax.Rate) / 100;
    }
}
```

To keep this example simple, the anonymous code snippet is as follows:

```
<< Anonymous Apex, 3 product, resued tax and Vendor >>
TaxBracket taxBracket = new TaxBracket( 'Sales',
    'Tax levied on all services provided', 10);

Vendor productVendor = new Vendor('Sunrise Electronics',
    'Sample Address', '123-456-7890', 'info@sunriseabc.com');

ProductWrapper product1 = new ProductWrapper('Amazon Echo',
    '6bygf686', 178, taxBracket, productVendor);

ProductWrapper product1 = new ProductWrapper('Kinivo Headset',
    '68y45h83', 34, taxBracket, productVendor);
```

The following figure shows the memory advantage of using the flyweight pattern in action. For the sake of simplicity, it is assumed that each variable in an object will take only 2 KB of memory; however, it actually depends on the data type:

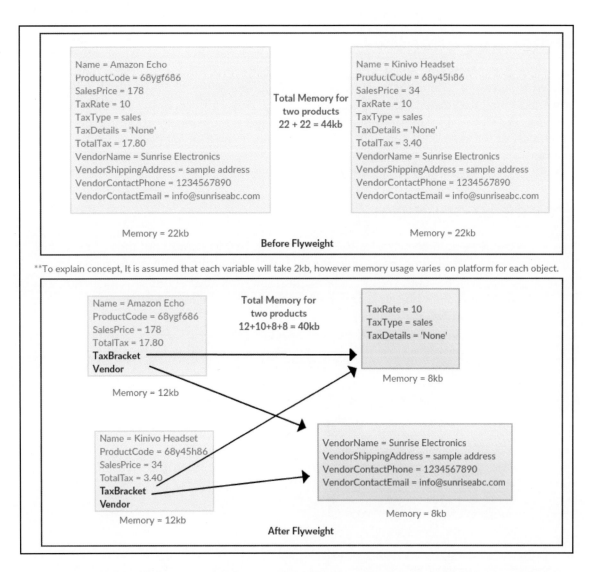

As seen in the preceding figure, there is a finite set of `TaxBrackets` and `Vendors` to be created and associated with multiple products, hence resulting in memory savings. Before using the flyweight pattern, it was 44 KB and after, it was 40 KB for two product records. If there are more product records, then the memory saving will be high.

Alternatively, flyweight objects are instantiated via the factory method with additional logic to ensure that no duplicate instances are created. Factories can store all the objects and return objects from the collection whenever a repetitive request is received.

Other use cases

Consider 50 contacts who share 10 Accounts in Salesforce. If we query these 50 contacts and a few properties of parent accounts in a single SOQL query, the `Account` object will be repeated for all the related contacts resulting in high consumption of the available *heap memory*. The flyweight pattern can be used here by querying contacts and accounts separately and then linking them. It will consume one extra SOQL but saves precious heap memory.

Points to consider

- All flyweight objects should be immutable, that is, should not incur any change during its lifetime, as an object is shared across multiple clients (objects).
- A flyweight object should only include common and repetitive data attributes and any (other objects using the flyweight objects) client-specific property should be maintained at client level.
- The flyweight design pattern focuses on creating small objects, but the facade pattern focuses on creating a single object to represent the whole ecosystem.

Summary

In this chapter we discussed ways in which we can structure our code to increase performance or mitigate incompatibilities between classes or create modular code.

The following table summarizes the structural design patterns:

Design pattern	Summary
The faÃ§ade pattern	This provides a simple interface for the existing complex functionalities
The adapter pattern	This helps in communication between two incompatible existing classes
The bridge pattern	This helps in communication between two classes, which are under heavy modification
The composite pattern	This enables unified access to a part and part-whole hierarchy
The decorator pattern	This adds capabilities to an existing class without changing its behavior
The flyweight patern	This improves the memory usage using shared objects

4

Behavioral Patterns

In the preceding chapters, we discussed how we can create objects or structure our code to enhance its modularity and reusability. This chapter focuses on design patterns to enable communication between objects and keep them loosely coupled at the same time.

Introducing these design patterns in code increases their flexibility and reusability in order to carry out the communication between objects. It mostly focuses on how an object interacts and how responsibilities are shared amongst them.

We should consider using behavioral patterns in the following scenarios:

- Passing same request to multiple handlers
- Implementing object-oriented callbacks
- Persisting and recovering the state of an object
- Parsing languages or defined scripts
- Sending a state notification to multiple recipients
- Defining a family of algorithms and using them interchangeably

In this chapter, we will discuss the following design patterns:

- The chain of responsibility pattern
- The command pattern
- The interpreter pattern
- The iterator pattern
- The mediator pattern
- The memento pattern
- The observer pattern
- The state pattern
- The strategy pattern
- The visitor pattern

The chain of responsibility pattern

It is a common situation where we need to debug or log some important information in Apex. It can help improve error handling and reporting or analyzing runtime errors while customers are using the application.

Apex provides the following debug levels from the lowest to the highest:

- NONE
- ERROR
- WARN
- INFO
- DEBUG
- FINE
- FINER
- FINEST

The preceding log levels are cumulative, which means that if the log level is DEBUG, then it will also include ERROR, WARN, and INFO.

Chapter 4

There is much more to learn about this topic; however, it would not be possible to cover it entirely in this chapter. Refer to the Salesforce help link to read more about it
at `https://help.salesforce.com/apex/HTViewHelpDoc?id=code_s etting_debug_log_levels.htm&language=en`.

Salesforce provides various debug methods in the `System` class, as shown in the following code:

```
//Option 1
 System.debug("Your debug message");
```

Or you can also use the following code:

```
//Option 2
System.debug(Logginglevel," Your debug Message");
```

It is recommended that you use the overridden `debug` method (option 2) where we can provide `Logginglevel` parameter as well. Developers often face problems wherein they do not find the complete log information. This is due to the 2 MB log size limit set by the Force.com platform.

Primarily, developers can configure the debug logging level for Apex, workflow, validation rule, and so on at the user or class level. But, it may not be adequate in some scenarios. For example, when there is a huge code base with lots of `debug` statements. In such scenarios, defining `Logginglevel` in `debug` statements can help you get more granular control of debug logs.

Using debug statements is one of the most basic ways to analyze errors in Apex. Additionally, developers employ other mechanisms such as sending error notifications, saving error information in a custom object, and so on.

Each logging mechanism has its own separate approach to handle error information. It is recommended that we should structure our code to achieve a low cohesion and reusability.

The chain of responsibility pattern focuses on avoiding tight coupling between sender and receiver objects to handle requests. It allows chaining of multiple *receiving* objects to give a chance to more than one object to handle the same request. It follows the *launch and leave* design with a single execution path, allowing more than one object to process the request.

The following diagram explains the chain of responsibility pattern at a high level:

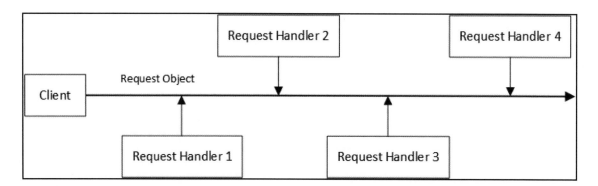

Let's try to solve this problem using the chain of responsibility design pattern.

Sending e-mails via the Apex code can hit the governor limit (1,000 e-mails allowed per 24 hours) if e-mails are sent to an external user. Also, while inserting a log record in a custom object can hit the governor limit (number of DML statements in a single transaction).

Let's create a custom object named Debug to store debug logs. It contains two fields: title and message. The title field is created as an **external Id** to make it an indexed field.

Marking the field as **external Id** allows it to be indexed; to improve the performance of related SOQL queries, list view, global search, and reports.

The following screenshot shows the object structure:

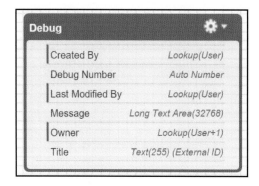

We plan to handle `debug` statements in the following three different ways:

- Send error notifications
- Insert a log record in a custom object
- Add log messages to the standard debug log

As per the **single responsibility principle**, we will need to create three separate classes for each of the preceding functionalities. Each of these classes will share some common logic, which can be implemented in the base class. This is an opportune moment to create an **abstract** class.

The abstract class includes the following parameters:

- Constants to define log levels
- The `setNextLogger` method to define the next handler in the chain
- The `logMessage` method to decide whether the current and next log handler in the chain needs to be invoked on the basis of the requested log level
- The `write` abstract method, which needs to be implemented by all handlers (child classes):

```
public abstract class RequestHandler{
    /* constant for debug log */
    public static final integer LOG_LEVEL_SYSTEMDEBUG = 1;
    /* constant error and warn */
    public static final integer LOG_LEVEL_SAVE = 2;
    /* constant for Send Email */
    public static final integer LOG_LEVEL_EMAIL = 3;
    /* Requested log level */
    protected integer handlerLogLevel ;
    /* Link to next Request Handler object */
    protected RequestHandler nextLogger;
    /* Set next Logger Request Handler class*/
    public void setNextLogger(RequestHandler logger){
        this.nextLogger = logger;
    }
    // "Chaining" of log request handlers
    public void logMessage(integer level, String message){
        if(handlerLogLevel <= level){
            write(message);
        }
        /* "Chain" - Pass request to next Request Handler object*/
        if(nextLogger != null){
            nextLogger.logMessage(level,message);
        }
    }
}
```

```
    //This method needs to be implemented by all child log handlers
    abstract protected void write(String message);
}
```

Here, we have the first concrete class, which extends the `RequestHandler` abstract class to display the message in the standard debug logs:

```
public class RequestHandler_SystemDebug extends RequestHandler{
    public RequestHandler_SystemDebug(integer log_level){
        this.handlerLogLevel = log_level ;
    }
    /**
     * This Debug Request Handler class only
     * log Debug messages in Log Console
     * */
    public override void write(String message){
        System.debug(message) ;
    }
}
```

The second request handler class is used to save messages in a `Debug__c` custom object so that it can be used later for reporting purposes.

Saving debug records in the database has many pitfalls, which are as follows:

- It uses the Salesforce data storage
- Possibilities of hitting DML limits
- The DML statement cannot be invoked from constructors

```
public classRequestHandler_Save extends RequestHandler{

    public RequestHandler_Save(integer log_level){
        this.handlerLogLevel = log_level ;
    }
    /**
     * This Debug Request Handler class Saves
     * Debug log record in custom object for
     * future error analysis.
     * */
    public override void write(String message){
        //Peform Database operation only if we have DML statement limit
available
        if(Limits.getLimitDMLStatements() - Limits.getDMLStatements() > 1 )
        {
            //Perform Database operation only if we have atleast 1 row
limit available for DML
            if(Limits.getLimitDMLRows() - Limits.getDMLRows() > 1){
```

```
                /**
                 * Save first 250 characters in "title" field
                 * as its indexed , so searching will be fast
                 * */
                String title = message.length() > 250 ? message.left(249) :
message ;
                Debug__c debugObj = new Debug__c(Title__c = title,
Message__c = message);
                insert debugObj ;
            }else{
                System.debug(LoggingLevel.ERROR,'DML row limit exhausted');
                System.debug(LoggingLevel.ERROR, message);
            }
        }
        else{
            System.debug(LoggingLevel.ERROR,'DML statement limit
exhausted');
            System.debug(LoggingLevel.ERROR, message);
        }
    }
}
```

The following request handler provides a functionality to send e-mail notifications:

```
public class RequestHandler_SendEmail extends RequestHandler{
    public RequestHandler_SendEmail(integer log_level){
        this.handlerLogLevel = log_level ;
    }
    /**
     * Send Email to Salesforce User.
     * We would not be sending email to external users to avoid governor
limits
     * */
    public override void write(String message){
        try
        {
            List<Messaging.SingleEmailMessage> lstEmailstoSend =
                new List<Messaging.SingleEmailMessage>();
            //read usernames from Custom label which has
//comma seperated users name
            for(User u : [SELECT ID FROM User WHERE UserName IN :
                System.Label.Developer_User_Name.split(',')]){

                Messaging.SingleEmailMessage emailMessage =
new Messaging.SingleEmailMessage();

                emailMessage.setSubject('Debug Message from Salesforce');
```

```
                    emailMessage.setTargetObjectId(u.Id);
                    emailMessage.setPlainTextBody(message);
                    emailMessage.setSaveAsActivity(false);
                    lstEmailstoSend.add(emailMessage);
            }
            if(!lstEmailstoSend.isEmpty())
                Messaging.sendEmail(lstEmailstoSend);
        }catch(Exception e){
            System.debug(LoggingLevel.ERROR,'Some error occurred while
sending email for Logging purpose');
            System.debug(LoggingLevel.ERROR, e.getMessage());
        }
    }
}
```

Now, we need a utility class that will create a chain of all the preceding logger requests that we created earlier, as shown in the following class:

```
public class Loggers{
    /**
     * Below method returns Chained Loggers
     * */
    public static RequestHandler getChainOfLoggers(){
        RequestHandler debugLogger = new
RequestHandler_SystemDebug(RequestHandler.LOG_LEVEL_SYSTEMDEBUG);
        RequestHandler databaseLogger = new
RequestHandler_Save(RequestHandler.LOG_LEVEL_SAVE);
        RequestHandler emailLogger = new
RequestHandler_SendEmail(RequestHandler.LOG_LEVEL_EMAIL);
        //Create Chain of Loggers
        //DebugLogger -> Database Save -> Send Email

        debugLogger.setNextLogger(databaseLogger);
        databaseLogger.setNextLogger(emailLogger);
        //return logger which starts chain
        return debugLogger;
    }
}
```

The following figure depicts the flow of the chain of responsibility pattern:

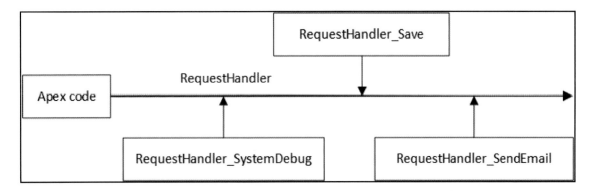

The following are the code snippets used to verify a functionality.

Sample code 1:

```
RequestHandler logger = Loggers.getChainOfLoggers();
logger.logMessage(RequestHandler.LOG_LEVEL_SYSTEMDEBUG, 'I am logger using
Chain of responsibility principal');
```

Behavior:

The log level in the preceding code snippet is set to LOG_LEVEL_SYSTEMDEBUG (value 1). Therefore, the logMessage method of the RequestHandler abstract class will only execute request handlers that have the log level less than or equal to LOG_LEVEL_SYSTEMDEBUG. In this case, the RequestHandler_SystemDebug handler will be executed.

Output:

- The message will be printed on the debug log

Sample code 2:

```
RequestHandler logger = Loggers.getChainOfLoggers();
logger.logMessage(RequestHandler. LOG_LEVEL_SAVE, 'I am logger using Chain
of responsibility principal');
```

Behavior:

The log level in the preceding code snippet is set to LOG_LEVEL_SAVE (value 2). In this case, the RequestHandler_SystemDebug and RequestHandler_Save handlers will be executed.

Output:

- The message will be printed on the debug log
- The message will be saved in a Debug__c custom object

Sample code 3:

```
RequestHandler logger = Loggers.getChainOfLoggers();
logger.logMessage(RequestHandler. LOG_LEVEL_EMAIL, 'I am logger using Chain
of responsibility principal');
```

Behavior:

The log level in the preceding code snippet is set to LOG_LEVEL_EMAIL (value 3). In this case, the RequestHandler_SystemDebug, RequestHandler_Save, andRequestHandler_SendEmail handlers will be executed.

Output:

- The message will be printed on the debug log
- The message will be saved in a Debug__c custom object
- An e-mail will be sent to all users saved in the custom label

The following diagram is a class diagram for our final code:

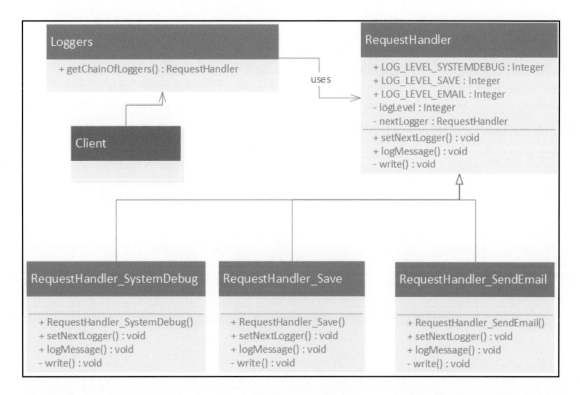

As discussed in the previous design pattern, we learnt a new way to decouple a request and a series of receiver objects, and at the same time recursively call all request handlers, which know how to process a request. This is very powerful and one of the most common behavioral design patterns used.

Points to consider

- The chain of responsibilityaddresses how you can decouple senders and receivers
- The chain of responsibility passes a sender request along with a chain of potential receivers

The command pattern

While designing various frameworks (or APIs), it is a common requirement for developers to want client(s) to extend the capabilities of the framework and plug in their specific business functionalities, which can work in conjunction with the framework functionality. This approach can be very beneficial to clients as it allows them to add their specific business logic to the framework and attune all the functionalities as per their business needs.

At Universal Call Center, the team realized that the functionality being built can be packaged as an `AppExchange` package for a wider reach. The team started laying out a high-level approach and soon hit a roadblock. An application needs to have a bulk data processing capability to be fulfilled by an Apex batch process. However, on completion of the batch process execution, the application is expected to invoke a client-specific post-processing functionality.

The team plans to develop a factory method implementation to enable the core system (an `AppExchange` package) to use the client's module (a client-specific functionality), if required. The following diagram depicts the proposed architecture:

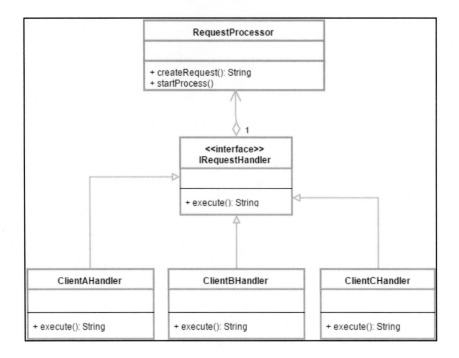

However, soon everyone realized that it is not a scalable model. It will result in the `AppExchange` application being modified for each client. This is not practical and does not serve the purpose of the application. They identified that it will be beneficial to allow clients to be able to implement their required business functionalities, and hence extend the `AppExchange` app. This approach will allow clients to implement and design their functionalities as they desire. Also, it keeps the client-specific functionality out of the `AppExchange` app, which further helps in making a more generic product.

Consider an `AppExchange` package; the challenge was to identify how an `AppExchange` application can be designed to be customizable for each customer with the least effort. The team realized that the problem lies in the separation of the functionality from its invocation; that is, *what* is to be done and *when* to do it.

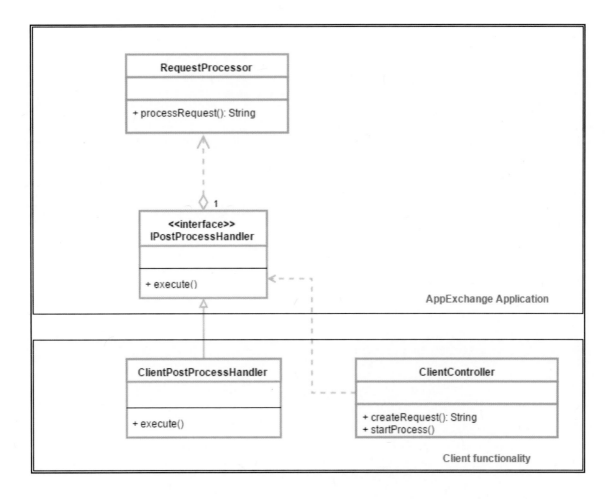

Note that the important point here is *what* is to be done and *when* to do it. A requestor knows *what* is to be done and provides the information to the receiver. A receiver on the other hand just knows *when* it has to be done and invokes the process appropriately.

This design approach is referred to as the **command design pattern**. The command design pattern allows you to abstract the behavior as an object, that is, the action/method is exposed as an object. So, the requestor provides an instance of a command to the receiver (the receiver has no knowledge of the requestor). A receiver just invokes the command to complete the required process.

 The **command design pattern** helps you create an instance for an operation, thereby enabling it to be passed and queued.

So, while developing the `AppExchange` application, the team needs to develop `PaymentReconciliationBatch` and expose `IRequestHandler` so that each client can implement a custom functionality, as desired, to be invoked by `PaymentReconciliationBatch` appropriately.

The following is the `AppExchange` application's code for the `IRequestHandler` command interface and the `PaymentReconcilliationBatch` class (which receives and executes the command):

```
/**
 * Interface to expose capability for client to implement and provide
 * to AppExchange app for invocation
 */

public interface IRequestHandler {
    void execute();
}

/**
 * Batch process within AppExchange app
 */
public class PaymentReconciliationBatch
    implements Database.Batchable<Sobject>, Database.Stateful{
    IRequestHandler passhandler;
    IRequestHandler failhandler;
    //constructor
    public PaymentReconciliationBatch(IRequestHandler passhandler,
                                      IRequestHandler failhandler){
        this.passhandler = passhandler;
```

```
        this.failhandler = failhandler;
    }
    public Database.QueryLocator start(
      Database.BatchableContext jobId){
      //query to retrieve required records
      return Database.getQueryLocator(
          'select id from Account limit 100');
    }
    public Void execute(Database.BatchableContext jobId,
                        List<sObject> recordList){
      //data processing logic
    }
    public Void finish(Database.BatchableContext jobId){
        try{
         //invoke success command
         passhandler.execute();
      }
        catch(Exception ex){
         //invoke error command
            failhandler.execute();
        }
    }
}
```

Now, wherever this `AppExchange` application is installed, client team can implement `IRequestHandler` interface and create a client-specific command handler, as per their business needs.

The following are the commands that each client team can develop within their respective Salesforce organizations to extend the capabilities of a package:

```
//Command to handle success
public class SuccessHandler implements IRequestHandler{
    public void execute(){
        system.debug('** Successful operation');
    }
}

//Command to handle failure
public class FailureHandler implements IRequestHandler{
    public void execute(){
        system.debug('Failure operation');
    }
}
```

With the preceding command classes, a client can execute the
`PaymentReconcilliationBatch` batch class and provide it with appropriate commands
(`SuccessHandler` and `FailureHandler`). The following is a code snippet to test our
example:

```
//create commands
IRequestHandler passhandler = new SuccessHandler();
IRequestHandler failhandler = new FailureHandler();

//create instance of batch process
PaymentReconciliationBatch objbatch =
    new PaymentReconciliationBatch(passhandler, failhandler);

//execute batch process
Database.executeBatch(objbatch);
```

The output of the preceding code snippet is as follows:

```
** Successful operation
```

This approach helps us ensure that the `AppExchange` code has only a generic functionality
and any client-specific functionality is kept within the client organization only.

So, practically, when we have two clients, that is, ABC Corp and XYZ Inc, using this
`AppExchange` package, the high-level class diagram will be as follows:

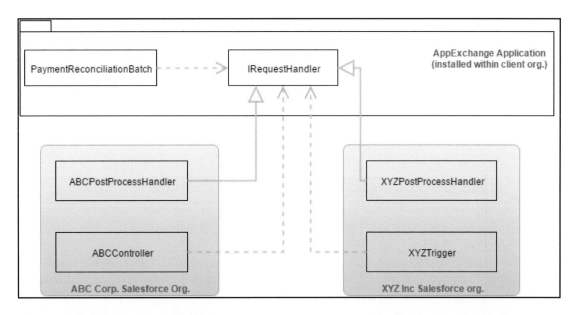

So, both ABC Corp and XYZ Inc have extended the AppExchange package by adding their business functionalities. At the same time, the AppExchange package is a generic application, catering uniformly to both the clients.

The command design pattern, by virtue of its ability to separate the method/process logic from its invocation, is used in myriads of scenarios. For example:

- **Undo operations**: The command design pattern can be used to abstract all the commands and provide a very transparent way to apply or revert an action.
- **GUI interfaces**: These are event handlers for various UI controls, for example, a button click, hover, and so on. The command pattern helps in queuing multiple commands for the same event, for example, if multiple actions are to be performed on a button click.
- **Parallel processing**: Here, each command is sent to a common processor/server from where it is sent to distributed systems/threads for processing (a master/slave scenario).

Some points to note

- The command design pattern separates a requestor from a receiver so that a receiver can invoke the process without knowing the requestor. Also, the process can be invoked at a different time from the submission.
- The command pattern can be used to create a macro-like functionality wherein each individual command is stored, logged, and repeated in a given order.

The interpreter pattern

With all the new age features being incorporated in the system of Universal Call Center, the team starts getting ambitious and wants to add more flexibility for the users. There are some support processes related to the media industry and they have a very peculiar problem. In the media industry, the copyright date is mostly displayed as roman numerals. This becomes very difficult for call center agents to comprehend copyright dates. As you can imagine, it can be a tedious job for any person to convert a roman number to a decimal number. So, the team decided to automate the process of converting roman numerals into decimal numbers programmatically for faster customer issue resolutions.

Here is an example of a roman numeral and its equivalent decimal values:

- *I = 1*
- *V = 5*
- *MCMXCVIII = 1998*

Easier said than done! The team realized that the calculations and permutations involved are huge and can lead to a very complex code. Roman numerals are interpreted based on their character's position and interpretation. The team unanimously identified that they will need to create a parser, which can read the input value (roman numerals) and generate the decimal numbers as the output.

Team tries to again look at design patterns for help, where they can have a repetitive process of parsing roman numerals, and convert the value to the decimal system.

 The **interpreter pattern** helps in designing a code structure to interpret a language by dividing the language into various grammatical constructs.

The interpreter pattern fits right into this premise. It helps in designing a solution wherein a script or language needs to be interpreted (hence the name interpreter).

The interpreter pattern consists of the following classes:

- `AbstractExpression`: This is the abstract class or interface containing the `interpret` method used for all grammar expressions.
- `TerminalExpression`: This is the leaf-level class, which represents individual expressions. For example, roman numerals I, V, and X.
- `NonTerminalExpression`: This connects two or more terminal expressions and interprets child expressions (hierarchical nonterminal expressions) by iterating over an entire child tree, for example, AND, OR, NOT, and so on.
- `Context`: This is used to pass data and share results between interpreting the class hierarchy.

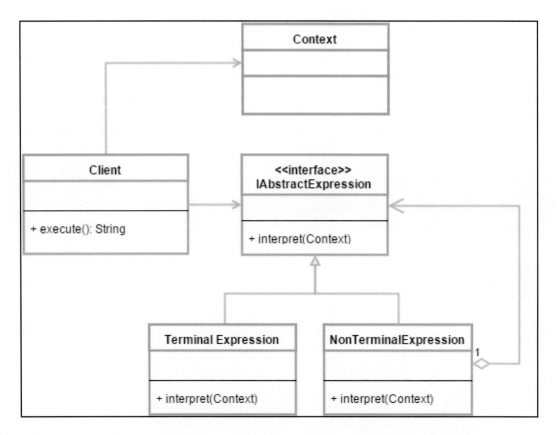

The use of terminal expressions and nonterminal expressions is totally subjective with regard to the language construction; for example, creating an interpreter for a programming language will require both terminal expressions as well as nonterminal expressions. In the case of a roman numeral interpretation, nonterminal expressions are not required as they do not contain any joining expressions such as AND, OR, and so on.

Team used the following code with the interpreter design pattern to convert roman numerals into decimal numbers.

The following code is a `context` class:

```
/**
 * Context class to pass input and output values
 * */

public class Context {
    public String Input {get; set;}
    public Integer Output {get; set;}
    public Context(String input){
        this.Input = input;
    }
}
```

The following class represents the `AbstractExpression` class of the interpreter pattern containing the `interpret` method:

```
/**
 * Abstract expression class for interpreter
 * */

public abstract class AbstractExpression {
    public void interpret(Context context){
        if(String.isBlank(context.Input)) return;
        if(context.Input.startsWith(Nine())){
            context.Output += 9 * Multiplier();
            context.Input = context.Input.substring(2);
        }
        else if(context.Input.startsWith(Five())){
            context.Output += 5 * Multiplier();
            context.Input = context.Input.substring(1);
        }
        else if(context.Input.startsWith(Four())){
            context.Output += 4 * Multiplier();
            context.Input = context.Input.substring(2);
        }
        while(context.Input.startsWith(One())){
            if(context.Output == null) context.Output = 0;
            context.Output += 1 * Multiplier();
            context.Input = context.Input.substring(1);
        }
    }
    public abstract String One();
    public abstract String Four();
    public abstract String Five();
    public abstract String Nine();
    public abstract Integer Multiplier();
}
```

The following classes represent terminal expression classes for roman numerals where *M = 1000*:

```
/**
 * Roman thousand expression (M = 1000)
 * */

public class RomanThousandExpression extends AbstractExpression{
    public override String One() { return 'M'; }
    public override String Four(){ return ' '; } //no expression for four
thousand
    public override String Five(){ return ' '; } //no expression for five
thousand
    public override String Nine(){ return ' '; } //no expression for nine
thousand
    public override Integer Multiplier() { return 1000; } // decimal
multiplier for thousandth decimal place

}
```

The following class represents a nonterminal expression class for hundreds, where *C = 100, CD = 400, D = 500*, and *CM = 900*:

```
/**
 * Roman hundred expression
 * */

public class RomanHundredExpression extends AbstractExpression{
    public override String One() { return 'C'; }
    public override String Four(){ return 'CD'; }
    public override String Five(){ return 'D'; }
    public override String Nine(){ return 'CM'; }
    //decimal multiplier for hundredth decimal place
    public override Integer Multiplier() { return 100; }

}
```

The following class represents a nonterminal expression class for tens, where *X = 10, XL = 40, L = 50*, and *XC = 90*:

```
/**
 * Roman Ten expression (X = 10)
 * */

public class RomanTenExpression extends AbstractExpression{
    public override String One() { return 'X'; }
    public override String Four(){ return 'XL'; }
    public override String Five(){ return 'L'; }
```

```
    public override String Nine(){ return 'XC'; }
    public override Integer Multiplier() { return 10; } //decimal
multiplier for tenth decimal place


}
```

The following class represents a nonterminal expression class for numbers less than 10, where *I = 1, IV = 4, V = 5,* and *IX = 9*:

```
/**
 * Roman One expression
 * */

public class RomanOneExpression extends AbstractExpression{
    public override String One() { return 'I'; }
    public override String Four(){ return 'IV'; }
    public override String Five(){ return 'V'; }
    public override String Nine(){ return 'IX'; }
    public override Integer Multiplier() { return 1; } //decimal multiplier
for unit decimal place
}
```

The following class shows you the interpreter pattern in action by acting as a controller for the Visualforce page:

```
/**
 * Demo class for Interpreter design pattern
 */

public class InterpreterDemoController{

    public Context DemoContext {get; set;}
    public String RomanNumberToConvert {get; set;}
    public InterpreterDemoController(){
        DemoContext = new Context('');
    }
    public void convertToDecimal(){
        DemoContext = new Context(RomanNumberToConvert);
        DemoContext.Output = 0;
        // Build roman numerals grammar
        List<AbstractExpression> romanExpressionGrammar = new
List<AbstractExpression>();
        romanExpressionGrammar.add(new RomanThousandExpression());
        romanExpressionGrammar.add(new RomanHundredExpression());
        romanExpressionGrammar.add(new RomanTenExpression());
        romanExpressionGrammar.add(new RomanOneExpression());
        // Interpret roman numberals
        for (AbstractExpression expression :romanExpressionGrammar)
```

```
        {
            expression.interpret(DemoContext);
        }
    }
}
```

The following Visualforce page converts roman numerals into decimal numbers using the interpreter pattern:

```
<apex:page controller="InterpreterDemoController">
    <apex:form >
        <apex:pageBlock >
            <apex:pageblockSection >
                <apex:pageblockSectionItem >
                    <b>Roman number</b>
                    <apex:inputtext value="{!RomanNumberToConvert}" />
                </apex:pageblockSectionItem>
                <apex:pageblockSectionItem >
                    <b>Decimal number</b>
                    <apex:outputtext value="{!DemoContext.Output}" />
                </apex:pageblockSectionItem>
            </apex:pageblockSection>
            <apex:pageblockButtons >
                <apex:commandButton value="Convert"
action="{!convertToDecimal}"/>
            </apex:pageblockButtons>
        </apex:pageBlock>
    </apex:form>
</apex:page>
```

The following image shows the output of our example:

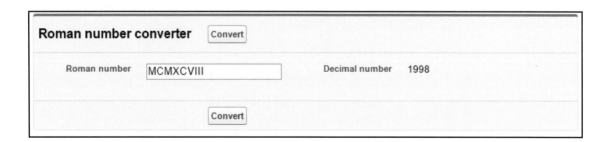

The following image is the final class diagram of our solution:

Points to consider

- An interpreter is often confused with composite as they seem to be similar. However, an interpreter can be considered as an abstract factory of composite. An interpreter is basically a large group of classes, designed to interpret a language. However, a composite is a structure of classes used to make similar classes work together with ease.
- An interpreter can be nonrecursive (as in the preceding example) as opposed to a composite.

The iterator pattern

Developers of *Universal Call Center* are given the task of displaying a customer banner on the service cloud. This banner should display the account name and ticker symbol of a customer. This functionality needs to be reusable so the team decides to use a newly launched Salesforce lightning platform to create a banner component. An expected requirement is to display one account at a time. Team discussed an approach to retrieve all the required accounts and display them in a sequence. However, as this would result in lots of records being stored in the browser memory, this solution is not memory-efficient. So, the team identifies that they need a solution wherein they can retrieve one account at a time.

The **iterator pattern** is the right fit for this use case. It allows sequential iteration of a collection of records.

 The **iterator pattern** provides a way to access the elements in a collection sequentially without exposing its underlying data structure. The iterator pattern promotes the idea of *full object status* to traverse a collection present in that object.

In older television sets, viewers had to manually set the frequency to connect to a required channel. This required a viewer to scan through all the available frequencies, irrespective of whether they had a channel transmission or not. It would be a better experience to allow the viewer to automatically jump to frequencies having valid channel transmissions. This can be achieved by iterators, which hide unused frequencies and show the next frequency with a channel transmission. Something similar is done by modern-day television remotes, whereby they automatically switch to the next available channel on a single button click.

An implementation of this design pattern mostly introduces two interfaces: one for a container, which returns an iterator object and another, which actually defines methods to navigate the collection.

The following class diagram shows, in general, the implementation of the iterator pattern:

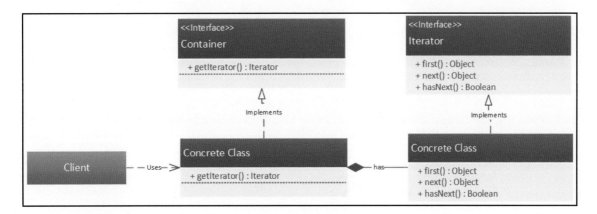

The following is the iterator interface, which needs to be implemented by the Apex class to support iteration features:

```
/**
* interface to be implemented by iterator
**/
public interface Iiterator {
    boolean hasNext();
     Object next();
    void setCurentIndex(Integer index);
}
```

If needed, we can implement many other methods, such as `first()`, `last()`, and `prev()` to navigate on the first, last, or previous element.

Normally, in the iterator pattern, we maintain the current index of an item in a collection at class level. However, for the lightning component to invoke the Apex method, it needs to be declared as **static**. Declaring a class as **static** in the Force.com platform means that the class cannot maintain its state (values of a variable) between multiple user requests. We have additionally used the `setCurrentIndex()` method in the interface so that we can maintain its state at client-side (the lightning component) and send it to the Apex method in each user request.

The following interface is for a container class that will return an instance of the iterator class:

```
/**
* interface to be implemented by container
**/
public interface IContainer {
    IIterator getIterator();
}
```

Let's start implementing a concrete class in Apex, which will implement the preceding interfaces:

```
public class AccountIterator implements IIterator{
        List<Account> lstAccount ;
        integer currentIndex = 0;
        public void setCurentIndex(Integer index){
            currentIndex = index;
        }
        public AccountIterator(List<Account> lstAcc ){
            this.lstAccount = lstAcc;
        }
        public boolean hasNext(){
            if(currentIndex < lstAccount.size())
            {
                return true;
            }
            return false;
        }
        public Object next(){
            return lstAccount[currentIndex];
        }
    }
```

The preceding Apex class implements the `IIterator` interface to support the navigation of an item in the list of accounts.

The following Apex class is used to implement the `IContainer` interface, which will return an instance of the `AccountIterator` iterator class.

```
public class AccountContainer implements IContainer {
    public IIterator getIterator(){
        List<Account> lstAcc = [SELECT ID, Name, TickerSymbol FROM Account
LIMIT 50000] ;
        return new AccountIterator(lstAcc);
    }
}
```

In the preceding Apex class, we are instantiating and returning the `AccountIterator` class with a list of accounts.

Until this point, we have already implemented the iterator pattern. Now, we need to plug this into the lightning component as a banner to display the account name and ticker information. We need to create the Apex controller class to be used by.

Let's create a server-side controller (the Apex controller) for our lightning component, which will use the iterator pattern to check whether the next element exists and return the next account from the list:

```
public class AccountIteratorController {
    @AuraEnabled
    public static String getAccount(Integer index){
        IIterator accntIterator = new AccountContainer().getIterator();
        if(index == null)
            index = 0;
        accntIterator.setCurentIndex(Integer.valueOf(index));
        if(accntIterator.hasNext())
        {
            return JSON.serialize(accntIterator.next());
        }
        return 'empty';
    }
}
```

The `getAccount` method is marked as static and annotated by `@AuraEnabled`.

> If we want to access any Apex method from the lightning component, then it should be marked with the `@AuraEnabled` annotation.

The `getAccount` method accepts the current item's index (maintained in the client-side lightning component) and passes it to a controller class. It returns the next account record as a JSON string. If there are no more records in the collection, then the controller returns a string with the `empty` value.

Now, all our ground work is completed. We just need to invoke the preceding class from the lightning component and see it in action.

We will start with the component to display an image from the Salesforce image library. This is an SVG image, and therefore, it cannot be used to simply with the image (`img`) element of HTML.

Why use SVG images?
SVG images are vector graphics, which provide the ability to use the same images across multiple resolutions without distorting the image quality, unlike widely used image formats, such as JPEG, PNG, GIF, and so on.

Salesforce has recently released the **Salesforce Lightning Design System (SLDS)** as open source; this provides all CSS and images used to create the standard lightning component itself. So, instead of rewriting CSS again for our component, we will use it from SLDS.

We need to download and upload SLDS in a static resource from `https:/
/developer.salesforce.com/lightning/design-system`.

We will use the SVG component from trailhead to display an icon from SLDS.

You can read more about how to create a lightning component to display SVG images in this trailhead module at `https://developer.s
alesforce.com/trailhead/project/slds-lightning-components
-workshop/slds-lc-4`.

Let's start with the lightning component, which will use the `AccountIteratorController` Apex class to display the account as a banner using the iterator pattern:

```
<aura:component controller="AccountIteratorController" >
  <aura:attribute name="accountName" type="String" />
  <aura:attribute name="accountSymbol" type="String" />
  <aura:attribute name="currentIndex" type="Integer" />
  <aura:handler name="init" value="{!this}" action="{!c.doInit}" />
  <div class="container">
    <div class="slds-grid
          slds-wrap
             slds-grid--align-center">
    <div class="slds-col">
      <span class="slds-icon__container
                slds-icon-standard-account
                slds-icon__container--circle">
        <c:svg class="slds-icon--large"
         xlinkHref="/resource/SLDS/assets/icons/standard-
sprite/svg/symbols.svg#account"/>
        <span class="slds-assistive-text">
           Client Icon
        </span>
      </span>
    </div>
```

```
      <div class="slds-col slds-p-left--x-small">
      <div id="AccountName">
        {!v.accountName}
      </div>
        <div id="AccountAddress">
        {!v.accountSymbol}
      </div>
        <div class="button slds-p-top--large">
        <button aura:id="btnNext"
            class="slds-button slds-button--destructive slds-button--small"
            onclick="{!c.getNext}" data="{!v.currentIndex}">
          Next
        </button>
      </div>
      </div>
    </div>
    </div>
</aura:component>
```

In the preceding component, we declared three attributes to display the account name and ticker symbol and maintained the index of the current element, which will be passed to the Apex controller class with each request. This component also declares an event handler to call the doInit() method in the client-side controller (AccountIteratorControler.js) when the component is loaded in a browser.

The following code represents the JavaScript controller, AccountIteratorControler, for the lightning component. As a best practice, we should only use the JavaScript controller to delegate methods to the helper file of the component so that code maintenance is easy:

```
({
    getNext : function(component, event, helper) {
        helper.getNextItem(component);
    },
     doInit : function(component, event, helper) {
        helper.getNextItem(component);
    }
})
```

The following code is written in the `AccountIterator.js` helper file where all the heavy lifting to call the Apex method and response handling (callback) is implemented:

```
({
    getNextItem : function(component) {
        //Apex method to be executed
        var action = component.get("c.getAccount");
        //Index of current item in banner
        var curInd = component.get("v.currentIndex");
        if(isNaN(curInd)){
            curInd = 0;
        }
        action.setParams({
            index : curInd
        });
        //handle response from
        action.setCallback(this, function(actionResult) {
            var retVal = actionResult.getReturnValue() ;
            if(retVal == 'empty')
            {
                //No more data in list so restart
                curInd = 0 ;
                component.set("v.currentIndex",
                            curInd);
                this.getNextItem(component);
            }else{
                var jsonObj = JSON.parse(retVal);
                var curInd = component.get("v.currentIndex") ;
                if(isNaN(curInd)){
                    curInd = 0;
                }
                curInd = 0 + curInd + 1;
                //show Acount Name
                component.set("v.accountName",
                            jsonObj.Name);
                //show Ticker symbol
                component.set("v.accountSymbol",
                            jsonObj.TickerSymbol);
                //set index of current item
                component.set("v.currentIndex",
                            curInd);
            }
        });
        //invoke Apex controller method
        $A.enqueueAction(action);
    }
})
```

The `Component.get()` method is used to get the attribute defined in the component, and in the same way, `Component.set()` is used to set a value in the attribute defined in a component. The `$A.enqueueAction()` method adds Apex methods that need to be executed in a queue so that they can be executed asynchronously. The `$A.util.addClass()` is a JavaScript utility method provided by the lightning framework to add the CSS class to any component.

It's time to wrap the lightning component in an application and test our code.

The following code is part of the lightning application, which can be launched to see the actual output:

```
<aura:application >
    <ltng:require styles="/resource/SLDS/assets/styles/salesforce-
lightning-design-system-ltng.css" />
        <div class="slds">
            <c:AccountIterator />
        </div>
</aura:application>
```

The `ltng:require` tag is used to import a static resource in a lightning application.

The following screenshot shows the lightning component banner:

The following is a class diagram of a banner component:

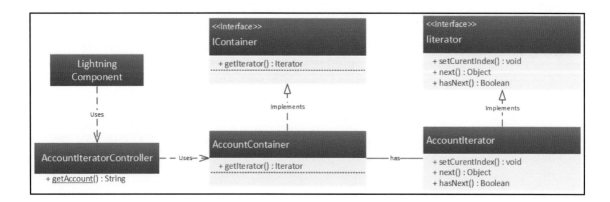

Apex supports the iterator pattern out of the box. It provides flexibility to create custom iterators by implementing an iterator interface. You can read more about how to implement a custom iterator in Apex at `https://developer.salesforce.com/docs/atlas.en-us.apexcode.meta/apexcode/apex_classes_iterable.htm`.

Points to consider

- Polymorphic iterators rely on factory methods to instantiate the appropriate iterator subclass
- An iterator can traverse a composite structure

The visitor pattern

A start-up company decided to create a music/song library application using Salesforce public sites and communities. Users can browse through thousands of songs, add them to the cart, and purchase them. There are many types of music genres available on websites, such as pop, rock, electronic, and so on. Prices are based on music genres; thus, during a checkout, the development team needs to maintain a list of different songs sold by genres and calculate the price accordingly. For the sake of simplicity, we will consider only three types of music in our example.

Developers decided that all the songs will share some common properties, such as a title and album name, and thus it makes sense to use inheritance. They developed the following abstract class that must be extended by all types of song/music:

```
public abstract class Music {
    protected String title;
    protected String album;
    public abstract String getMusicDetail();
}
```

The getMusicDetail() method, which is declared as an abstract, assumes that different operations need to be performed, depending on different types of music.

The following three classes have been created by developers for different types of music:

```
public class RockMusic extends Music{

    public  RockMusic(String title,  String album){
        this.title = title;
        this.album = album;
    }
    public override String getMusicDetail(){
        return 'Rock Music : Title - '+title+' ,album - '+album;
    }
}
public class PopMusic extends Music{

    public PopMusic(String title,  String album){
        this.title = title;
        this.album = album;
    }
    public override String getMusicDetail(){
        return 'Pop Music : Title - '+title+' ,album - '+album;
    }
}

public class ElectronicMusic extends Music{

    public ElectronicMusic(String title,  String album){
        this.title = title;
        this.album = album;
    }
    public override String getMusicDetail(){
        return 'Electronic Music : Title - '+title+
               ' ,album - '+album;
    }
}
```

As shown in the preceding code, all the classes extend the `Music` abstract class and implement their own version of the `getMusicDetail` methods.

Consider the following sample calculator class, showing the correct method being invoked:

```
public class MusicPriceCalculator {

    public static void calculatePrice(PopMusic m){
        System.debug('Calculate price of Pop Music') ;
    }
    public static void calculatePrice(RockMusic m){
        System.debug('Calculate price of Rock Music') ;
    }
    public static void calculatePrice(ElectronicMusic m){
        System.debug('Calculate price of Electronic Music') ;
    }
}
```

Now, assume that end users have added a few songs to their cart. The following code snippet shows the calculation of the price:

```
List<Music> lstMusic = new List<Music>();

lstMusic.add(new RockMusic('Go Johnny go',
                'Chuck Berry Is on Top'));

lstMusic.add(new PopMusic('When Doves Cry',
                'The Very Best Of Prince'));

lstMusic.add(new ElectronicMusic('Strobe',
                'For Lack of a Better Name'));
for(Music m : lstMusic){
    if(m instanceof PopMusic)
    {
        MusicPriceCalculator.calculatePrice((PopMusic)m) ;
    }else if(m instanceof RockMusic){
        MusicPriceCalculator.calculatePrice((RockMusic)m) ;
    } else if(m instanceof ElectronicMusic){
        MusicPriceCalculator.calculatePrice((ElectronicMusic)m) ;
    }
}
```

Running the preceding anonymous code will generate the following output:

```
Calculate price of Pop Music
Calculate price of Rock Music
Calculate price of Electronic Music
```

Assume that a new music category has been added, `PopRockMusic`, which is a child of `PopMusic`, so it becomes a grandchild of the `Music` class:

```
public virtual class PopRockMusic extends PopMusic{
    protected String title;
    protected String album;
    public PopRockMusic(String title,  String album){
        super(title,album);
        this.title = title;
        this.album = album;
    }
    public virtual override String getMusicDetail(){
        return 'Pop Rock Music : Title - '+title+' ,album - '+album;
    }
}
```

The updated `MusicPriceCalculator` will be as follows:

```
public class MusicPriceCalculator {

    public static void calculatePrice(PopMusic m){
        System.debug('Calculate price of Pop Music') ;
    }
    public static void calculatePrice(RockMusic m){
        System.debug('Calculate price of Rock Music') ;
    }
    public static void calculatePrice(ElectronicMusic m){
        System.debug('Calculate price of Electronic Music') ;
    }
    public static void calculatePrice(PopRockMusic m){
        System.debug('Calculate price of PopRock Music') ;
    }

}
```

Now, try to run the following anonymous code:

```
List<Music> lstMusic = new List<Music>();

lstMusic.add(new PopMusic('Pop Song',
                'Pop Album'));

lstMusic.add(new PopRockMusic('PopRock Song',
                'PopRock Album'));

for(Music m : lstMusic){
    if(m instanceof PopMusic)
    {
        MusicPriceCalculator.calculatePrice((PopMusic)m) ;
    }else if(m instanceof RockMusic){
        MusicPriceCalculator.calculatePrice((RockMusic)m) ;
    } else if(m instanceof ElectronicMusic){
        MusicPriceCalculator.calculatePrice((ElectronicMusic)m) ;
    }  else if(m instanceof PopRockMusic){
        MusicPriceCalculator.calculatePrice((PopRockMusic)m) ;
    }
}
```

The expected output is:

```
Calculate price of Pop Music
Calculate price of PopRock Music
```

However, the actual output is:

```
Calculate price of Pop Music
Calculate price of Pop Music //unexpected result
```

As we can see in the preceding output, both the music objects qualify as instances of the PopMusic class. Hence, both the times the overloaded calculatePrice method was called for the PopMusic input parameter.

The problems with the preceding code are as follows:

- Explicit type casting (from music to child classes) could result in an unexpected behavior (the double dispatch problem)
- If any new type of music is added to the application, then type casting needs to be checked and changed accordingly throughout the application

Before proceeding to the solution of the preceding problems, let's discuss **dispatching** in OOPs.

Single dispatch

Single dispatch is also known as virtual methods and we have seen it multiple times in a real-life scenario.

The following classes show simple inheritance in Apex:

```
public virtual class Car {
    public virtual void detail(){
        System.debug('Its Car');
    }
}

public class Honda extends Car{
    public override void detail(){
        System.debug('Its Honda');
    }
}
```

Let's try to run the following code as anonymous apex in developer console

```
Car obj = new Honda();
obj.detail();
```

It will print `Its Honda`, which means that at runtime, it will decide which method needs to be executed. Even though the type of object is declared as `Car`, but at runtime Apex is able to determine it *solely on the basis of its actual type* and thus it's known as **single-dispatch**.

Double-dispatch

Double dispatch is a mechanism in programming where a call to various methods of a concrete class is decided on the basis of two types of objects involved.

In addition to the preceding `Car` and `Honda` classes, let's add the following class for insurance:

```
public virtual class Insurance {
    public virtual void insure(Car c){
        System.debug('This is insurance for Car');
    }
    public virtual void insure(Honda c){
        System.debug('This is insurance for Honda');
    }
}
```

```
public class PaintInsurance extends Insurance {
    public override void insure(Car c){
        System.debug('This is Paint insurance for Car');
    }
    public override void insure(Honda c){
        System.debug('This is Paint insurance for Honda');
    }
}
```

Now, try to run this code in an anonymous window of the developer console:

```
Insurance ins = new PaintInsurance ();
Car obj = new Honda();
ins.insure(obj);
```

The expected output will be as follows:

```
"This is Paint insurance for Honda"
```

However, the actual output is as follows:

```
"This is Paint insurance for Car"
```

Note that in the preceding code, a method is chosen solely on the basis of the type of the ins(insurance) object and not on the basis of the obj(car) type. This happens because Apex and other programming languages, such as Java and C#, support **single-dispatch** but not **double-dispatch**.

The visitor pattern can be used to implement the double dispatch behavior to ensure that the system generates the desired output.

 The **visitor pattern** is used to separate the algorithm from the object structure on which it operates.

The advantage of this pattern is to add new operations to an object without modifying its structure. This pattern follows the open/close principle of design patterns, which represents *O* from SOLID, as discussed in the previous chapters.

In short, this pattern allows you to add functionalities to a family of related classes without modifying the class itself.

Let's come back to our music application example and see how we can resolve this problem using the visitor pattern.

Guidelines to implementing the visitor pattern

We need to follow these two points for the visitor pattern:

1. The visitor class should implement the `visit()` method, which will be called for every element of a data structure. In our case, we should implement the `visit()` method, which will be called by the `PopMusic`, `PopRockMusic`, `RockMusic`, and `ElectronicMusic` classes.

2. All classes on which an operation (the price calculation) needs to be performed should provide the `accept()` method to accept the visitor and pass itself as an argument to the visitor class.

Let's work on replacing `MusicPriceCalculator` with the visitor class. We will create an `IMusicVisitor` interface, which needs to be implemented by all visitor classes:

```
public interface IMusicVisitor {
    void visit(RockMusic music);
    void visit(PopMusic music);
    void visit(ElectronicMusic music);
    void visit(PopRockMusic music);
}
```

As we can see in the preceding interface, a concrete class needs to implement the `visit` method for all types of elements of a data structure.

The following code is a concrete class implementation of the `IMusicVisitor` interface, which calculates the price on the basis of the genre type:

```
public class MusicPriceVisitor  implements IMusicVisitor{
    public Double finalPrice = 0;
    public MusicPriceVisitor(){
    }
    public void visit(RockMusic music){
        System.debug('In Rock Music Algorithm');
        finalPrice += 2;
    }
    public void visit(PopMusic music){
        System.debug('In Pop Music Algorithm');
        finalPrice += 3;
    }
    public void visit(ElectronicMusic music){
        System.debug('In Electronic Music Algorithm');
        finalPrice += 4;
    }
    public void visit(PopRockMusic music){
        System.debug('In PopRock Music Algorithm');
```

```
            finalPrice += 2;
        }
    }
```

So far, we have completed the first part of the visitor pattern, which specifies that an external class needs to implement the `visit` method for all the required types to be supported.

Now, it's time to move to the second point, which states that all the types that need to perform an operation (invoke the algorithm) must provide the `accept` method, and therefore our `Music` abstract class will change to the following code:

```
public abstract class Music {
    protected String title;
    protected String album;
    public abstract String getMusicDetail();
    public abstract void accept(IMusicVisitor visitor);
}
```

In the same way, all concrete classes are refactored to introduce the `accept` method to support the visitor pattern:

```
public class RockMusic extends Music{

    public  RockMusic(String title,  String album){
        this.title = title;
        this.album = album;
    }
    public override String getMusicDetail(){
        return 'Rock Music : Title - '+title+' ,album - '+album;
    }
    public override void accept(IMusicVisitor visitor){
        visitor.visit(this);
    }
}
public class PopMusic extends Music{

    public PopMusic(String title,  String album){
        this.title = title;
        this.album = album;
    }
    public override String getMusicDetail(){
        return 'Pop Music : Title - '+title+' ,album - '+album;
    }
    public override void accept(IMusicVisitor visitor){
        visitor.visit(this);
    }
```

```
}
public class ElectronicMusic extends Music{

    public ElectronicMusic(String title,   String album){
        this.title = title;
        this.album = album;
    }
    public override String getMusicDetail(){
        return 'Electronic Music : Title - '+title+' ,album - '+album;
    }
    public override void accept(IMusicVisitor visitor){
        visitor.visit(this);
    }
}

public virtual class PopRockMusic extends PopMusic{
    protected String title;
    protected String album;
    public PopRockMusic(String title,   String album){
        super(title,album);
        this.title = title;
        this.album = album;
    }
    public virtual override String getMusicDetail(){
        return 'Pop Rock Music : Title - '+title+' ,album - '+album;
    }
    public virtual override void accept(IMusicVisitor visitor){
        visitor.visit(this);
    }
}
```

Now, we can solve the previously discussed double **dispatch problem** using the following code snippet:

```
List<Music> lstMusic = new List<Music>();
lstMusic.add(new RockMusic('Go Johnny go','Chuck Berry Is on Top'));
lstMusic.add(new PopMusic('When Doves Cry','The Very Best Of Prince'));
lstMusic.add(new ElectronicMusic('Strobe','For Lack of a Better Name'));
lstMusic.add(new PopRockMusic('Sweet Home Alabama','Second Helping'));

MusicPriceVisitor visitor = new MusicPriceVisitor();

for(Music m : lstMusic)
{
    m.accept(visitor);
}
System.debug('Final Amount - '+visitor.finalPrice);
```

The output is as follows:

```
In Rock Music Algorithm
In Pop Music Algorithm
In Electronic Music Algorithm
In PopRock Music Algorithm
Amount - 11.0
```

In the preceding output, we can see that the `PopRockMusic` method (algorithm) is correctly invoked and solved the double dispatch problem.

If in future, developers want to add a new set of algorithms, let's say to calculate tax or discounts, we simply need to create a new visitor class by implementing the `IMusicVisitor` interface. Concrete classes already have the `accept` method that allows new visitor classes to use them.

The following class diagram shows the complete implementation of our example:

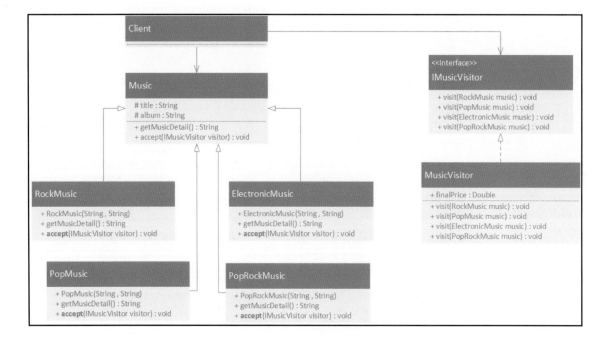

Points to consider

- Sometimes, the visitor class may require to access private members of the actual class, and you may be forced to change variables access to public.
- The order of iteration is not confirmed. As we can see, the `accept()` method is called on the basis of the existing collection of music. If you need to maintain the order of iteration like the first `RockMusic` process and then `PopMusic`, then this is not a suitable design pattern in this scenario.
- If the data structure is not confirmed, then this pattern is of no use. Slight changes in the data structure may result in rewriting the visitor class.
- If a new visitor (new music type) is added, then we need to update the visitor class to introduce operations on the new member.

The memento pattern

As the team progresses and is now focused on creating effective and efficient functionalities, Universal Call Center's management team decides to provide the sales team with a comprehensive functionality to generate quotes on the fly. The development team decided to create a Visualforce page within Salesforce to enable sales persons to generate quotes and present it to customers.

So, the team created a Visualforce page and controller to create a single page, which enables sales persons to select various products and generate quotes.

The following screenshot shows the final Visualforce page output created by developers:

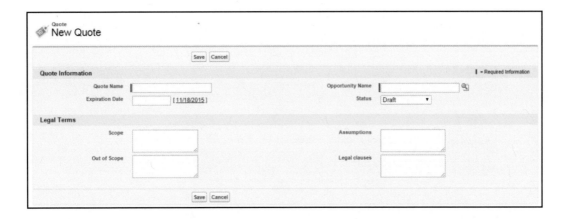

All was good until it was demonstrated to the sales team. The sales team specified that in their usual sales scenarios, they often need to generate multiple quotations for customers based on negotiations and need to revert to various versions. This was identified as a must-have requirement. So, the team went back to the drawing board. The problem was to identify a modular approach to provide sales persons with the ability to undo their work on a quote. A simple solution suggested was to store each quote state as a quote record (as per the standard Salesforce) but as it would mean more records, that is, more data usage, this approach was immediately rejected.

The team realized that they needed a design pattern to help them store the state of a quote on each change and then restore it or undo a state whenever required.

After much thought, they realized that the memento design pattern fulfills this requirement. It is something similar to Guy Pearce's movie *Memento*, where the protagonist has a terrible memory loss and has to depend on some notes/clues to remember various events.

Question: Why not simply create a list of controllers within a controller class to store the various states to facilitate an undo operation?
Answer: Practically it is possible, but it has three major issues.
Firstly, it is a very memory-consuming approach. Considering the various limits within Salesforce, it clearly is not an optimal choice.
Secondly, as this approach exposes each state externally, it violates the principle of encapsulation (the internal representation of an object should be hidden from outside access).
Thirdly, it does not allow you to persist and maintain specific attributes. Hence, it further impacts memory utilization.

The memento design pattern is extensively used to develop undo operations within applications. It helps divide the concerns involved, that is, a state to be maintained, maintenance of a state, and the usage of a state. In short, memento uses three types of constructs, which are as follows:

- **Caretaker:**
    - It maintains various memento objects to maintain a sequence and list of mementos
    - It handles "where" to be saved
- **Memento:**
    - An individual state to be maintained
    - It handles "what" to be saved

- **Originator**:
  - It uses a memento to persist its own state, and generates and consumes memento objects
  - It handles "how" and "when" to generate and use memento objects

 The **memento design pattern** is devised to handle scenarios where the internal state of the object is to be persisted at various points in time. It is just like keeping multiple versions to enable reverting to any previous version if needed.

The following image shows the class level diagram of the memento pattern:

Originator	Memento	CareTaker
	+ state : State	+ savedStates : List<Memento>
+ createMemento(): Memento + setMemento(Memento)		1 0..n

Let's start implementing the same application we discussed using the memento pattern.

Developers need to store and maintain various instances of memento (quote information) in a storage-efficient approach. So, they decided to convert all instances of memento to JSON and store them in a long text area field using the out-of-the-box JSON classes of Apex. Developers created a custom field in the standard `Quote` object of the long text area type named `State__c`.

The following is the Visualforce page code used to generate quotes with a newly added undo button to support versions:

```
<!-- Memento design pattern demo page -->
<apex:page controller="GenerateQuoteController ">
    <apex:form >
        <apex:sectionHeader  sub/>
        <apex:pageBlock mode="edit">
            <apex:pageBlockButtons >
                <apex:commandButton value="Save" action="{!save}"/>
                <apex:commandButton value="Undo" action="{!undo}"/>
                <apex:commandButton value="Cancel" action="{!cancel}"/>
            </apex:pageBlockButtons>
            <apex:pageBlockSection >
                <apex:inputfield value="{!Quote.Name}"/>
```

```
                    <apex:inputfield value="{!Quote.OpportunityID}"/>
                    <apex:inputfield value="{!Quote.ExpirationDate}"/>
                    <apex:inputfield value="{!Quote.Status}"/>
                </apex:pageBlockSection>
                <apex:pageBlockSection >
                    <apex:inputfield value="{!Quote.Scope__c}"/>
                    <apex:inputfield value="{!Quote.Assumptions__c}"/>
                    <apex:inputfield value="{!Quote.OutOfScope__c}"/>
                    <apex:inputfield value="{!Quote.LegalClauses__c}"/>
                </apex:pageBlockSection>
            </apex:pageBlock>
        </apex:form>
    </apex:page>
```

The following class represents `Memento` to maintain states:

```
/**
 * Memento class - stores state information
 * */
public class Memento {
    public Date ExpirationDate {get; set;}
    public String Status {get; set;}
    public String Assumptions {get; set;}
    public String OutOfScope {get; set;}
    public String LegalClauses {get; set;}
    public String Scope {get; set;}
}
```

The following code is the `CareTaker` class that contains a collection of `Memento` (states) and operations to add and retrieve memento versions:

```
/**
 * Maintains and manages various states
 * */
public class CareTaker {
    private List<Memento> lstMementos;
    private Integer currentLevel;
    public CareTaker(){
    }
    public CareTaker(String stateJson){
        CareTaker oldState = (CareTaker) Json.deserialize(stateJson,
CareTaker.class);
        this.lstMementos = oldState.lstMementos;
        this.currentLevel = oldState.lstMementos.size() - 1;
    }
    public void addState(Memento newState){
        if(lstMementos == null){
         lstMementos = new List<Memento>();
```

```
                currentLevel = 0;
        }
        else{
            if(currentLevel == null){
                currentLevel = lstMementos.size();
            }
            if(lstMementos.size() > currentLevel){
                List<Memento> newStates = new List<Memento>();
                for(Integer i=0; i < currentLevel; i++){
                    newStates.add(lstMementos[i]);
                }
                lstMementos = newStates;
            }
        }
        lstMementos.add(newState);
        currentLevel++;
    }
    public Memento getPreviousState(){
        Memento state = null;
        if(lstMementos != null && lstMementos.size() > 0){
            if(currentLevel == null){
                currentLevel = lstMementos.size() - 1;
            }
            if(lstMementos.size() > 0 && currentLevel >= 0){
                if(currentLevel > 0) currentLevel--;
                state = lstMementos.get(currentLevel);
            }
        }
        return state;
    }
}
```

The following controller class acts as an originator to provide undo operations by using
Memento and CareTaker.

```
/**
 * Originator for Memento Demo - handles generation of memento objects
 * */
public class GenerateQuoteController {
    CareTaker demoCareTaker;
    public Quote Quote {get; set;}
    public GenerateQuoteController(){
        String quoteId =
System.currentPageReference().getParameters().get('id');
        loadData(quoteId);
    }
    public void loadData(Id quoteID){
        demoCareTaker = new CareTaker();
```

```
        if(quote == null){
            quote = new Quote();
        }
        if(quoteID != null){
         quote = [select id, Name, OpportunityId , Assumptions__c,
ExpirationDate, LegalClauses__c, OutOfScope__c, Status, State__c, Scope__c
from quote where id = :quoteId];
            demoCareTaker = new CareTaker(quote.State__c);
        }
        else{
            //do nothing
        }
    }
    public void save(){
        saveState();
        upsert quote;
    }
    private Memento generateMemento(){
        Memento newState = new Memento();
        newState.Assumptions = quote.Assumptions__c;
        newState.ExpirationDate = quote.ExpirationDate;
        newState.LegalClauses = quote.LegalClauses__c;
        newState.OutOfScope = quote.OutOfScope__c;
        newState.Status = quote.Status;
        newState.Scope = quote.Scope__c;
        return newstate;
    }
    private void saveState(){
        //generate memento for current state
        Memento newstate = generateMemento();
        //add state to caretaker
        demoCareTaker.addState(newState);
        //searlize caretaker for persistence
        quote.State__c = Json.serialize(demoCareTaker);
    }
    private void restoreState(Memento state){
        quote.Assumptions__c = state.Assumptions;
        quote.ExpirationDate = state.ExpirationDate;
        quote.LegalClauses__c = state.LegalClauses;
        quote.OutOfScope__c = state.OutOfScope;
        quote.Status = state.Status;
        quote.Scope__c = state.Scope;
    }
    public void undo(){
        //retrieve old state
      Memento previousState = demoCareTaker.getPreviousState();
        //restore old state
        restoreState(previousState);
```

```
    }
    public void cancel(){
        //handle cancel button click
    }
}
```

Points to consider

- Often, command and memento are used together to achieve a complete undo-redo functionality. Command helps store action-related information and memento helps store the state at any given point of time.
- Flyweight and memento can be used (as described in the previous case) to avoid maintaining the state of unnecessary attributes.
- The memento pattern can be further optimized by storing only changes/additions in subsequent states. This can help reduce the memory footprint of state objects.

The observer pattern

This is a very common design pattern and can be seen being implemented in many areas of software applications, such as (**MVC**Model View Controller (MVC), event handling, and almost all GUI toolkits. If we take an example of MVC, then "View" informs all its dependents such as the controller whenever there is any change in the UI.

This design pattern is also referred to as the **publisher-subscriber pattern** frequently. It works on the principle of **don't call us – we'll call you**. The publisher, in this case, notifies all its subscribers whenever required.

 The observer pattern is a behavioral design pattern in which an object (a subject or publisher) maintains a list of all its dependents (an observer or subscriber) and notifies them whenever there is any change in its state.

Following are the thumb rules to implement the observer pattern:

- The `Subject` class maintains a list of all its dependent observers with additional methods, such as `subscribe`, `unsubscribe`, `notify`, and so on
- The `Observer` class mostly extends an `observable` class or interface containing the `update` or `notify` method called by the `Subject` class

Let's see this simple design pattern in action. We will consider the same example of the music library portal, as we discussed earlier in the visitor pattern. Customers search for songs that are not yet released to the public and are in the promo phase. So, developers want to allow customers to subscribe for e-mail notifications regarding a given song and to receive an e-mail when that song is released.

The following image shows the high-level object structure needed to maintain a list of all customers who want to receive e-mail notifications:

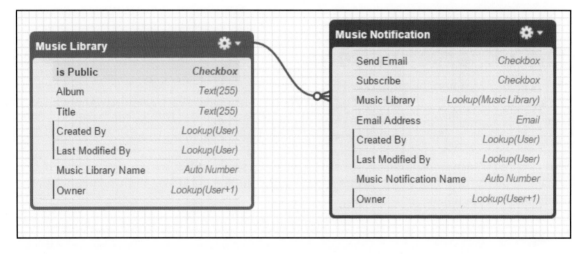

The `Music Library` object contains information about all the songs added on the portal that are available for purchase. The `is Public` checkbox indicates whether the music is released or not on the portal. In our example, we want to send e-mail notifications to all the customers maintained in the `Music Notification` object whenever songs are made public. The `Music Notification` object contains the e-mail address of a customer and the `Subscribe` checkbox indicates whether the end user wants to receive a notification.

Apex has a limit of 1,000 e-mails in 24 hours. So, we will be using workflow e-mails to bypass this limit.

We have to assume that the workflow rule is written on the `Music Notification` object. It says that whenever the `Send Email` field is changed and the value is `true`, then an e-mail notification is sent to all the subscribed customers.

Let's start with the `Subject` class, which will have the necessary methods to `subscribe`, `unsubscribe`, and `notify`:

```
public interface ISubject {
    void subscribe(Music_Notification__c observer);
    void unSubscribe(Music_Notification__c observer);
    void notifyObservers();
}
```

The following interface needs to be implemented by all the observers, which should be notified by a subject:

```
public interface IObserver {
    void notify();
}
```

The following class is a concrete implementation of `observer`, which gets a list of newly released songs and notifies all the customers who have subscribed to receive song notifications. In order to send an e-mail notification from the workflow rule, the `Send_Email__c` field is set to `true`:

```
public class MusicObserver implements IObserver{
    LIst<String> musicId ;
    // notify for passed music
    public MusicObserver(LIst<String> mId){
        musicId = mId;
    }
    public void notify(){
        List<Music_Notification__c> lstMusicNotify = [SELECT
ID FROM  Music_Notification__c  Where
Music_Library__c IN: musicId  AND
Subscribe__c = true] ;
        if(!lstMusicNotify.isEmpty())
        {
            for(Music_Notification__c mn : lstMusicNotify)
            {
                mn.Send_Email__c = true ;
```

```
            }
            //Workflow rule is written to send email if "Send_Email__c" is
    true
            update lstMusicNotify ;
        }
    }
}
```

The following class provides the subscribe and unsubscribe methods to allow observer instances to subscribe or unsubscribe from notifications. It also provides the notifyObservers method, which invokes the notify method of all the observers:

```
public class MusicSubject implements ISubject{
    LIst<String> musicId ;
    public MusicSubject(LIst<String> mId){
        musicId = mId ;
    }
    public void subscribe(Music_Notification__c observer)
    {
        observer.Subscribe__c = true;
        insert observer;
    }
    /**
     * Assuming parameter observer will only have email addres and music Id
     * */
    public void unSubscribe(Music_Notification__c observer)
    {
        List<Music_Notification__c> lstExistingSubsriber = [SELECT
            ID  FROM  Music_Notification__c  WHERE
            Email_Address__c = :observer.Email_Address__c
            AND Music_Library__c =: observer.Music_Library__c] ;
        if(!lstExistingSubsriber.isEmpty())
        {
            for(Music_Notification__c m : lstExistingSubsriber){
                m.Subscribe__c = false;
         }
            update lstExistingSubsriber ;
        }
    }
    public void notifyObservers()
    {
        IObserver obs = new MusicObserver(musicId);
        obs.notify();
    }
}
```

Whenever any song is made `public`, there will be a change in the database. Therefore, we can use triggers on the music record to inform all the subscribers:

```
trigger ObserverPatternStart on Music_Library__c (after update) {

    List<String> lstQualifiedSubjectIds = new List<String>();
    for(Integer i =0 ; i<Trigger.New.size() ; i++)
    {
        //If existing music is made public
        if(Trigger.new[i].is_Public__c && Trigger.new[i].is_Public__c !=
Trigger.old[i].is_Public__c){
            lstQualifiedSubjectIds.add(Trigger.new[i].id) ;
        }
    }
    if(!lstQualifiedSubjectIds.isEmpty())
    {
        MusicSubject sub = new MusicSubject(lstQualifiedSubjectIds);
        sub.notifyObservers();
    }
}
```

Let's summarize the preceding example:

- Users will navigate to the **Music Library**, and if they see that music is not `public`, then they will click on the **Subscribe** button, which internally calls the `subscribe()` method from `MusicSubject`.
- If the admin updates the `is Public` flag to `true` on a record of `Music Library`, then the trigger will execute to call the `notifyObservers()` method from the `MusicSubject` class.
- The `notifyObservers()` method will call the `notify()` method of the `MusicObserver` observer class. The `notify()` method will get all the related records from the database and update the field to trigger the workflow rule for an e-mail notification.

The following anonymous code shows the observer pattern in action:

```
//user navigates to album which is not yet public
List<MUSIC_LIBRARY__c> lstSongs = [SELECT ID FROM MUSIC_LIBRARY__c WHERE
Album__c = 'Chuck Berry Is on Top'];

List<Music_Notification__c> lstSubscriberlist = new
List<Music_Notification__c>();
for(MUSIC_LIBRARY__c song : lstSongs)
{
    Music_Notification__c notify = new
```

```
Music_Notification__c(Music_Library__c = song.Id,
    Email_Address__c = 'abc@xyz.com', Subscribe__c = true);
}

//user subscribes to album
insert lstSubscriberlist;

for(MUSIC_LIBRARY__c song : lstSongs)
{
    //make album public
    song.is_Public__c = true;
}

//changes made to database
update lstSongs;
```

The output is as follows:

```
trigger will execute notifyObservers() of MusicSubject
notify() of MusicObserver will be invoked to mark sendEmail field in
notification record
changing field "Send Email" will invoke Workflow rule to send email
```

The following class diagram shows the overall structure of a solution using the observer pattern:

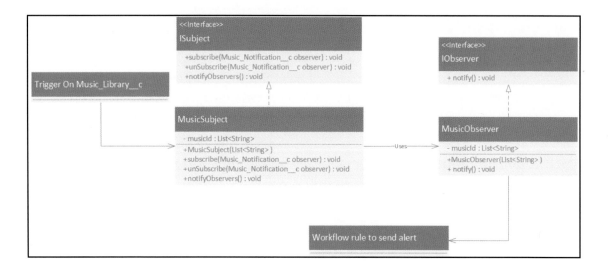

Point to consider

The observer pattern addresses how you can decouple senders and receivers, but with different trade-offs. Observer defines a decoupled interface that allows multiple receivers to be configured at runtime.

The state pattern

Having implemented so many patterns effectively, the Universal Call Center team is very excited and realizes that they can review its existing code and identify whether it can be remodeled effectively using appropriate design patterns.

One such interesting area identified by the team was to handle various case-related functionalities based on the case's status. For example, if the case has a status, new, then the case cannot be closed. If the case's status is Open, then the agent can create case comments and so on.

The team realized that the existing code for this functionality is not very scalable and is prone to issues. Currently, the code is placed in an if-else block and is highly nonmodular.

This is just a basic example to explain this scenario; however, other options, such as the validation or workflow rule, can be used to achieve this:

```
/**
 * Current class with non-modular code
 * */
public class CaseHelper {
    public void closeCase(Case customerCase){
        if(customerCase.Status == 'New'){
            //throw error as case cannot be closed if in stage "New"
        }
        else if(customerCase.Status == 'Open'){
            //validate agent has entered closure reason
        }
        else if(customerCase.Status == 'In Process'){
            //validate agent has sent email to customer
        }
        else if(customerCase.Status == 'Closed'){
            //throw error; case already closed
        }
        else{
            //automatically send email to case owner informing about case
closure
        }
```

```
        }
    }
```

As it is evident, this code is hard to maintain and scale up. Similarly, there are various other case-related features in the existing code base, where similar if-else blocks are used to identify the case stage and perform actions accordingly. Consider, if a new case stage is to be added, it could be a nightmare for the entire team, as the change will impact lots of existing Apex classes/triggers and will result in a comprehensive exercise.

 The key thing here is that the behavior of a functionality is dependent on the state of the object (case).

It would have been ideal for the functionalities to be abstract, and for the Apex classes/triggers to invoke processes without knowing about the case's status. This is where the state design pattern shines brightly.

 The *state design pattern* helps to encapsulate the state's specific behavior on an object.

The following is the class diagram of the state pattern:

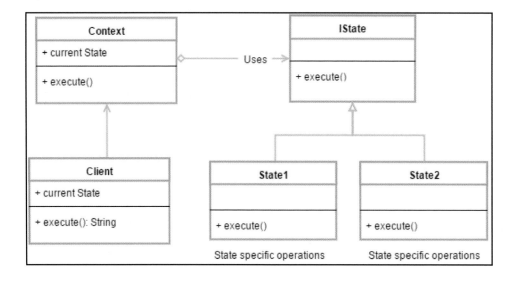

With the state design pattern, the client code (Apex classes/triggers) can be developed while being completely ignorant of the state (the case status) of object. This way, client code can be leaner and more abstract. As a result, the concrete class implementation of the IState interface is a container of all the functionalities of an object when an object is in a specific state(s). Client classes do not have any knowledge about the possible states and resulting behavior of the state classes. Client classes interact with an object uniformly, irrespective of the state of the object.

The following interface needs to be implemented by all concrete classes, which need to perform state-specific operations:

```
/**
 * Case state abstract class
 * */
public interface CaseState {
    void close(Case customerCase);
    void calculateTimeSpent(Case customerCase);
    void validate(Case customerCase);
}
```

The following concrete class handles the functionality related to cases with the New status:

```
/**
 * New case state handler
 */
public class NewCaseState implements CaseState{
    public void close(Case customerCase){
        system.debug('** close new case');
    }
    public void calculateTimeSpent(Case customerCase){
      //calculate time from date/time case was created
      system.debug
('** time calculation not applicable for new case');
    }
    public void validate(Case customerCase){
        system.debug('** validate new case');
    }
}
```

The following concrete class handles the functionality related to cases with the Open status:

```
/**
 * Open case state handler
 */
public class OpenCaseState implements CaseState{
    public void close(Case customerCase){
        system.debug('** close open case');
    }
    public void calculateTimeSpent(Case customerCase){
      //calculate time from date/time case status was set to "New"
      system.debug('** calculate time spent for open case');
    }
    public void validate(Case customerCase){
        system.debug('** validate open case');
    }
}
```

The following concrete class handles the functionality related to cases with the In Process status:

```
/**
 * In-Process case state handler
 */
public class InProcessCaseState implements CaseState{
    public void close(Case customerCase){
        system.debug('** close in-process case');
    }
    public void calculateTimeSpent(Case customerCase){
      //calculate time from date/time case status was set to "Open"
      system.debug('** calculate time spent for in-process case');
    }
    public void validate(Case customerCase){
        system.debug('** validate in-process case');
    }
}
```

The following concrete class handles the functionality related to cases with the `Closed` status :

```
/**
 * Closed case state handler
 */
public class ClosedCaseState implements CaseState{
    public void close(Case customerCase){
       system.debug('** Error - closed case cannot be closed');
    }
    public void calculateTimeSpent(Case customerCase){
       system.debug('** calculate time spent for close case');
    }
    public void validate(Case customerCase){
       system.debug('** Error - closed case cannot be validated');
    }
}
```

The following `Context` class handles all the interactions with state classes. It usually contains the logic to invoke state-specific classes and handles transitions from one state to another:

```
/**
 * Interface to case state handlers
 */
public class CaseContext {
    public CaseState State {get; set;}
    public CaseContext(String caseStatus){
        if(caseStatus == 'New'){
         this.State = new NewCaseState();
        }
        else if(caseStatus == 'Open'){
         this.State = new OpenCaseState();
        }
        else if(caseStatus == 'In Process'){
         this.State = new InProcessCaseState();
        }
        else if(caseStatus == 'New'){
         this.State = new ClosedCaseState();
        }
    }
    public void closeCase(Case customerCase){
        State.close(customerCase);
    }
    public void isValid(Case customerCase){
        State.validate(customerCase);
    }
}
```

```
/**
 * Interface to case state handlers
 */
public class CaseContext {
    public CaseState State {get; set;}
    public CaseContext(String caseStatus){
        if(caseStatus == 'New'){
         this.State = new NewCaseState();
        }
        else if(caseStatus == 'Open'){
         this.State = new OpenCaseState();
        }
        else if(caseStatus == 'In Process'){
         this.State = new InProcessCaseState();
        }
        else if(caseStatus == 'Closed'){
         this.State = new ClosedCaseState();
        }
    }
    public void close(Case customerCase){
        State.close(customerCase);
    }
    public void calculateTimeSpent(Case customerCase){
        State.calculateTimeSpent(customerCase);
    }
    public void validate(Case customerCase){
        State.validate(customerCase);
    }
}
```

The following code snippet shows the state pattern in action:

```
Case newCase = new Case(Status = 'New');
CaseContext context = new CaseContext(newCase.Status);

//calidate case
context.validate(newCase);

//set status to closed
newCase.Status = 'Closed';

//try closing a closed case
context = new CaseContext(newCase.Status);
context.close(newCase);
```

The following is the output generated:

```
** validate new case
** Error - closed case cannot be closed
```

Points to consider

The factory method pattern can be used along with the state pattern to hide the (abstract) creation of state implementations (state-specific classes).

The strategy pattern

This design pattern is also referred to as the **policy pattern** saying policy to be selected at runtime.

 The **strategy design pattern** is used to determine an algorithm at runtime to solve a problem.

We will continue with the example of the **Music Library** portal, as discussed in the visitor pattern and observer pattern. As part of the implementation, developers want to add support for payment in the shopping cart. However, the customer's selected payment type can be known only during a checkout. Customers can use either a credit card, debit card, or PayPal. Let's see how the strategy pattern can come in handy in this situation.

For this example, let's consider the following structure for a song (a **Music Library** custom object), which can be added to the shopping cart:

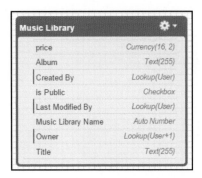

The following interface needs to be implemented by all the payment methods so that it can be selected at runtime:

```
/*
* This interface needs to be implemented by all classes
 * of Payment types which needs to be decided at runtime
 * */
public interface PaymentStrategy {
    void pay(Double amount);
}
```

The following concrete class implements the PaymentStrategy interface to process the payment using credit cards:

```
/*
* This class is used to pay using credit card
 * */
public class CreditCardStrategy implements PaymentStrategy{
    private String name;
    private String cardNumber;
    private String cvv;
    private String dateOfExpiry;
    /* Constructor */
    public CreditCardStrategy(String name, String cardNumber, String cvv,
String dateOfExpiry){
        this.name = name;
        this.cardNumber = cardNumber;
        this.cvv = cvv;
        this.dateOfExpiry = dateOfExpiry;
    }
    /* method from inteface PaymentStrategy */
    public void pay(Double amount){
        System.debug('Web service callout to pay using credit card') ;
    }
}
```

The following concrete class implements the `PaymentStrategy` interface to process the payment using PayPal:

```
/*
* This class is used to pay using Paypal
* */
public class PaypalStrategy implements PaymentStrategy{
    private String emailId ;
    private String password;
    /* Constructor */
    public PaypalStrategy(String emailId , String password){
        this.emailId = emailId;
        this.password = password;
    }
    /* Overrided method from inteface PaymentStrategy */
    public void pay(Double amount){
        System.debug('Web service callout to pay using paypal Account') ;
    }
}
```

The following concrete class implements the `PaymentStrategy` interface to process the payment using debit cards:

```
/*
* This class is used to pay using debit card
* */
public class DebitCardStrategy implements PaymentStrategy{
    private String name;
    private String cardNumber;
    private String pin;
    /* Constructor */
    public DebitCardStrategy(String name, String cardNumber, String pin){
        this.name = name;
        this.cardNumber = cardNumber;
        this.pin = pin;
    }
    /* method from inteface PaymentStrategy */
    public void pay(Double amount){
        System.debug('Web service callout to pay using Debit Card') ;
    }
}
```

The following class is used to add or remove songs in the shopping cart, and initiate the payment process:

```
/*
* This class is used calculate payment amount
 * */
public class ShoppingCart {
    List<Music_Library__c> lstSongs ;
    /*Constructor*/
    public ShoppingCart()
    {
        lstSongs = new List<Music_Library__c>();
    }
    /* Add music in cart */
    public void addSong(Music_Library__c m){
        lstSongs.add(m);
    }
    /* Remove music song from cart */
    public void removeSong(Music_Library__c songToRemove){
        Integer index = -1 ;
        for(Music_Library__c m : lstSongs)
        {
            index ++;
            if(m.Id == songToRemove.Id){
                lstSongs.remove(index);
                break ;
            }
        }
    }
    /* Calculate total amount and pay using selected mechanism*/
    public void pay(PaymentStrategy payMethod){
        Double finalAmount = 0;
        for(Music_Library__c m : lstSongs)
        {
            finalAmount = finalAmount+m.price__c ;
        }
        System.debug('Total amount to be paid - '+finalAmount) ;
        payMethod.pay(finalAmount) ;
    }
}
```

Let's create a sample record first in the `Music_Library__c` object by running the following code in an anonymous Apex:

```
List<Music_Library__c> lstSongs = new List<Music_Library__c>();
lstSongs.add(new Music_Library__c(Title__c='Go Johnny go',
                                  Album__c='Chuck Berry Is on Top',
                                  price__c= 2.0));

lstSongs.add(new Music_Library__c(Title__c='When Doves Cry',
                                  Album__c='The Very Best Of Prince',
                                  price__c= 2.5));

lstSongs.add(new Music_Library__c(Title__c='Strobe',
                                  Album__c='For Lack of a Better Name',
                                  price__c= 2.0));

insert lstSongs ;
```

Assume that the preceding three songs are added to the shopping cart of a user and they want to make a payment using a credit card. The following code can be executed in an anonymous window of the developer console to see how it works:

```
List<Music_Library__c> lstSongs = [SELECT ID,price__c FROM Music_Library__c
LIMIT 3] ;

ShoppingCart cart = new ShoppingCart();
for(Music_Library__c m : lstSongs)
{
    cart.addSong(m) ;
}

cart.pay(new CreditCardStrategy('Customer Name', '1234567891234567', '123',
'11/2016'));
```

The output will be as follows:

```
Total amount to be paid - 6.5
Web service callout to pay using credit card
```

In the same way, if we want to pay using PayPal, then we only need to change one line that calls the `pay()` methods, as shown in the following code:

```
List<Music_Library__c> lstSongs = [SELECT ID,price__c FROM Music_Library__c
LIMIT 3] ;

ShoppingCart cart = new ShoppingCart();
for(Music_Library__c m : lstSongs)
{
    cart.addSong(m) ;
}
cart.pay(new PaypalStrategy('abc@xyz.com', 'StrongPwd' ));
```

The output is as follows:

```
Total amount to be paid - 6.5
Web service callout to pay using PayPal Account
```

The following class diagram shows the overall structure of classes that we have used:

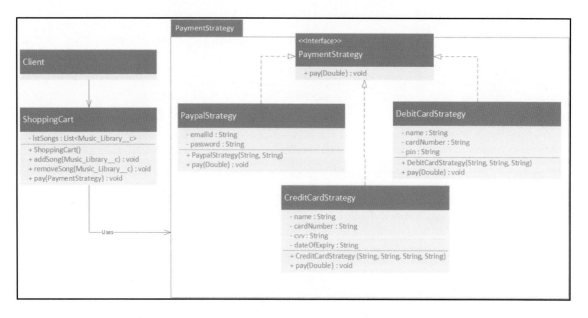

As we have seen in the preceding example, it is very easy to choose a payment method (algorithm) at runtime using the strategy pattern.

Points to consider

- The state pattern is like the strategy pattern except in its intent.
- The strategy pattern lets you change the core of an object. However, the decorator pattern lets you change the skin (wrapper).

Summary

This chapter focuses on how the behavior of an application can be changed during runtime to achieve flexibility, modularity, and scalability. The following table shows you a summary of behavioral design patterns discussed in this chapter:

Design pattern	Summary
Chain of responsibility	Chaining multiple handlers to process the same request
Command	Creating an object of an operation to be invoked at a later time
Interpreter	Interpreting a language
Visitor	Handling problems associated with double dispatch
Memento	Storing various versions of an object
Observer	Sending notifications to all subscribers
State	Encapsulating state-specific operations
Strategy	Choosing an algorithm at runtime

5

Handling Concurrency in Apex

We have discussed many design patterns of different categories such as creational, structural, and behavioral in the previous chapters. In this chapter, we will specifically discuss **concurrency** issues that can arise in code and see how to avoid these issues using **the** active object design pattern.

Understanding concurrency issues

In software applications, concurrency is the ability of an application to execute multiple processes simultaneously. While executing simultaneously, these processes can use shared resources and could potentially end up with data corruption or the wrong data.

We will try to understand concurrency issues using a real-life example of driving a car on a road. The following figure shows a two-lane driving road:

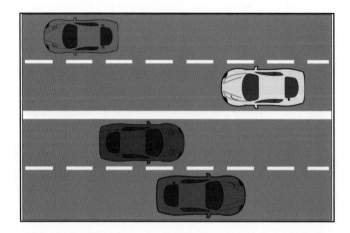

In the preceding figure, a car represents a process and a driving lane represents a shared resource. Driving on a straight road (without using a shared resource) is not a complex task. Complexities will arise when a driver of the car (a process) tries to change lanes (access a shared resource) and make sure that there is no chance of an accident (data loss or corruption). So, here we are trying to state that if a car (a process) runs on its own lane (not a shared resource), the possibility of data corruption is very low.

The following figure shows another scenario of a driving situation when lanes cross each other:

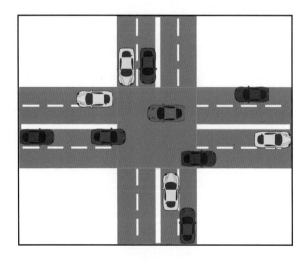

As we can see in the preceding figure, when a lane (a shared resource) is supposed to be used by multiple car drivers (processes), the chance of accidents (data loss) is very high, and everyone has to be extra careful while driving in such a scenario.

Apex is not like other languages, such as Java or C#, where one thread can communicate with the other threads. Due to this, many design patterns, such as the singleton pattern, or programming concepts, such as static variables, will not be helpful in Apex. To learn more about static variables in other languages, its state is maintained from the start of the program until the end of an application server (JVM/CLR for Java/C#). However, in Apex, the state of a static variable is maintained only within a single user request cycle. Once the processing of a user request is over, static variables are reset.

 Thread is the lightweight approach to implement parallel execution. In Apex, it can be related to future methods and batch Apex classes.

When we talk about multithreading, be aware that Apex does not really support it. There is no equivalent Apex class that is similar to the Java language class called `Thread`. We can execute a piece of work asynchronously using future methods, a queueable interface, a scheduler, or a batch Apex class.

So far, we have discussed that Apex supports asynchronous operations where these operations do not share memory data. It reduces a lot of our complexities and problems.

However, we have to be very careful with database records being simultaneously accessed by multiple processes.

In most cases, concurrency problems are very complex to identify and reproduce. Two processes trying to manipulate the same record in a database is not common. Chances could be a little bit higher in high traffic Salesforce implementations, where multiple users, and automated jobs perform data manipulation on the same datasets. The best approach in this situation is to avoid it completely and this can be achieved only by designs.

Reproducing concurrency problems in Apex

Let's try to understand and reproduce a concurrency issue in Salesforce. In this chapter, we will take an example of a nonprofit firm, which is funded by many corporates. The fund information is saved in a custom object named fund account. This nonprofit company is in the process of going online and currently does not support a fund transfer using online payment gateways. Interested volunteers of different companies need to call the organization's contact number to provide information about their contributions. The custom object fund account stores the aggregated contributions of all the employees of a company. Now, the foundation has been set up; let's look at a simple case of a concurrency issue.

The following figure shows the schema of the custom object fund account:

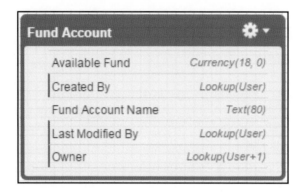

Two employees of the company *ABC* call the customer service of this nonprofit organization at the same time. The already available fund of the company *ABC* is $10,000 and both the employees want to contribute $100 more.

The **Edit** button of the fund account is overridden using the Visualforce page, and the save operation is done in a custom controller.

Two customer service representatives open the edit page of the fund account record for the company *ABC* at the same time. They do not know that the same record is opened by them for editing. Both of them can see the available fund as $10,000 and try to add $100 more. Both the representatives are able to save the record without any error or warning, and the final value is $10,100, which is wrong. The correct and expected value is supposed to be $10,200.

The following figure shows the concurrency problem that we just discussed:

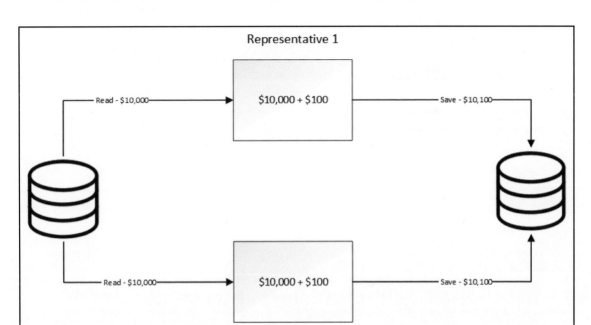

As we can see in the preceding figure, there is no error or warning and data is already corrupt.

 This situation is also known as the **race condition**. No one is ever going to notice it and there is no easy way to correct it as well. The reason for this corrupt data is the Apex controller, which we used to override the standard edit page. Apex is not concurrency safe until we design it.

However, the standard Salesforce interface is intelligent and can easily handle the preceding scenario. Standard Salesforce will throw an error to the other representatives trying to save the record saying that some other user already modified it. The following figure shows an error thrown by the standard Salesforce edit page:

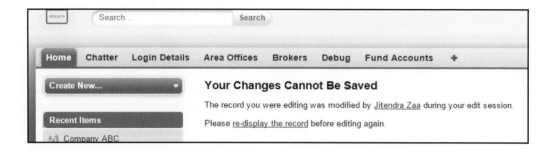

 Salesforce will throw a concurrency error only if the same record is being edited by different users; however, it will not throw an error if the same record is being edited by the same user from multiple processes, such as the standard Salesforce UI and from the Apex scheduler.

Let's generate a concurrency issue using the Apex code with the help of the following example.

In order to replicate this situation, we need to pause the execution for some time. As Salesforce does not have a thread-related class, so there is no native way to put the execution to sleep. After multiple trial and error methods, we came up with the following Apex class to pause the execution. Basically, we are using the Date class to add and subtract the days and year; as per our previous experience, date operations are a little bit slower:

```
/**
 *  This class is used to pause execution
 *
 */
public class Timer {
    //method to pause execution by n sec
    public static void pause(Integer seconds){

        Date todaysDate = Date.today();

        for(integer i = 0; i<8900*seconds; i++)
        {

            todaysDate.addYears(1).addDays(1).addMonths(1).addYears(-1);

        }

    }

}
```

The preceding `Timer` class consists of the `pause` static method that takes the *number of seconds* as the input parameter and performs a time-consuming operation to give the effect of a pause. We identified that if we repeatedly add and subtract the date 8,900 times, it could result in a 1 sec delay; however, there is no guarantee of precision, although we are pretty sure that it will work in most cases.

To create a concurrency situation, we need to start multiple processes at the same time, working on the same record. We observed that future methods are executed as soon as they get queued for execution. So, let's create a future method to update the same fund account:

```
/**
 * class to reproduce concurrency issue
 */
public class FundOperations {

    @future
    public static void addFund(String accountName, Decimal amount, Integer pause_second){

        List<Fund_Account__c> lstfundAcc = [SELECT Available_Fund__c FROM Fund_Account__c WHERE NAME =: accountName LIMIT 1];

        if(!lstfundAcc.isEmpty())

        {
            //pause execution
            Timer.pause(pause_second);

            lstfundAcc[0].Available_Fund__c = lstfundAcc[0].Available_Fund__c + amount;

            update lstfundAcc;

        }

    }

}
```

The `addFund` future method takes the following three arguments:

- An account name that needs to be updated
- The Amount that needs to be added to the existing fund
- The Pause duration (in seconds)

Let's execute the following anonymous code:

```
FundOperations.addFund('Company ABC',100,4);

FundOperations.addFund('Company ABC',100,4);
```

The preceding anonymous Apex code adds two future methods to update the fund account of the company *ABC* with $100 each. Also, we have specified a pause of 4 seconds.

After reading the record from the database, the execution is put to sleep for 4 seconds. In the meantime, the other future method will also read the same record and sleep for 4 seconds. At this point, both threads have retrieved the same information (that is, the available fund is equal to $10,000) from the database, and after 4 secs sleep, they will update and commit data. Both future methods will update the value as the available fund is equal to the sum of 10,000 and 100, that is, 10,100.

As we can see, the second future method will overwrite the amount added by the first future method with no error and warning. The expected output is $10,200. However, after the execution of the preceding code, the output would be $10,100.

The active object pattern

To overcome the preceding race condition in concurrency, we can use the active object pattern.

 The active object pattern decouples the method execution from its invocation. Mostly, the active object pattern executes in asynchronous mode. Requesters submit a task as an object in a queue, and a scheduler picks an object from the queue and executes its logic. An object in the queue knows what to do when invoked, and that's the reason why the name of the pattern is active object.

As Apex does not support multithreading, we cannot create a shareable queue, which can be accessed by multiple threads simultaneously; and therefore, we will do it with the help of the `Pending_Request__c` custom object. This custom object will save all the necessary information of the pending tasks that need to be performed asynchronously by the active object pattern.

 Do not confuse a shareable queue with the Salesforce queue. Here, a queue means a list of objects available in memory that can be accessed by multiple processes that are running.

The following figure represents the object schema of the custom object pending request:

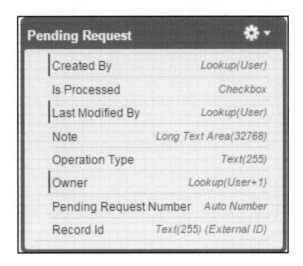

The custom object pending request consists of the following fields:

- **Is Processed**: This checkbox represents the record that is already processed.
- **Note**: This is a long text area field that can be used to add information about the success or error of processing.
- **Operation type**: This field will help an object know which operation needs to be performed on it. It could be adding funds, removing funds, and so on. We can have multiple services or handler classes to perform different types of operations on an object. The service class will process only the respective records that it can handle.
- **Record Id**: This is an external ID field so that the SOQL filter runs faster, which will represent a 15- or 18-digit ID of a record.

We will create a class that will act as an active object named `FundingAccount_ActiveObject`. It will contain the `performAddOperation()` method, which contains the logic for adding the amount to the fund account record:

```
/**
 *  This class will work as an Active Object and
 *  it known what operation needs to be performed
 *  when it is invoked.
 */

public class FundingAccount_ActiveObject {
    private Fund_Account__c obj ;
    private Decimal amountTobeAdded ;
    //Constructor
    public FundingAccount_ActiveObject(Fund_Account__c obj, Decimal
amount){
        this.obj = obj;
        this.amountTobeAdded = amount;
    }
    //This method knows what operation to perform
    public void performAddOperation(){
        if(amountTobeAdded != null)
            obj.Available_Fund__c = obj.Available_Fund__c + amountTobeAdded
;
    }
}
```

In general, while implementing the active object pattern, we need to have a service class. This service class should be thread-safe, containing methods to enqueue and dequeue records to be processed. This class can also be set up to automatically pull and process records from the queue continuously.

However, Apex is a language, which runs on the multi-tenant architecture, and because of governor limits, it is not recommended to have a scheduler listen continuously for a queue change. In our example, let's decouple the scheduling part and create a service class, which can be called from Apex asynchronously, to process pending requests in the queue (the `Pending_Request__c` object):

```
/**
 * This service class will be invoked from Scheduler to perform
 * operation on Active Object  to add fund.
 */
public class AddFund_Service_ActiveObject {
  //This method can be called from scheduler
  public void execute() {
    //List of Active objects
    List<Fund_Account__c> lstFundAccount = new List<Fund_Account__c>();
```

```
//Map to store QueueId for FundingAccount ID.
//It will be used to know whether record is processed or not
Map<Id,Id> mpFundAccountId_PendingAccountId = new Map<Id,Id>();

//Read Queue for "Add_Amount" type of operation
List<Pending_Request__c> lstPendingRequests = [SELECT Id,
   Record_Id__c,Parameter1__c FROM Pending_Request__c WHERE
   Is_Processed__c = false AND Operation_Type__c =
   'Add_Amount' LIMIT 2000];

//Create collection of Id to query Fund Account from queue
Map<Id,String> mpAccountParams = new Map<Id,String>();
for(Pending_Request__c pr :lstPendingRequests){
   //Parameter1__c contains amount to be added
   mpAccountParams.put(pr.Record_Id__c, pr.Parameter1__c);
   mpFundAccountId_PendingAccountId.put( pr.Record_Id__c, pr.Id);
}

//Get lock on records to avoid Race condition using "For Update"
 List<Fund_Account__c> lstAcnt = [SELECT ID , Available_Fund__c
    FROM Fund_Account__c WHERE ID IN :mpAccountParams.keySet()
    FOR Update];

//Ask Active object to take care of processing
 for(Fund_Account__c fund : lstAcnt){
    FundingAccount_ActiveObject activeObject = new
      FundingAccount_ActiveObject(
      fund,Decimal.valueOf(mpAccountParams.get(fund.Id)));
    activeObject.performAddOperation();

    //Active object performed operation but not committed yet in SFDC
    //This approach helps avoiding Governor limit error
    lstFundAccount.add(fund);
 }
 //commit to database and process result
 if(!lstFundAccount.isEmpty()) {
    List<Database.SaveResult> updateResults =
      Database.update(lstFundAccount , false);
    processResult(updateResults, mpFundAccountId_PendingAccountId);
 }
}
/* * This method takes Database.SaveResult list and prepares
 * success and error messages
 */
private void processResult(List<Database.SaveResult> updateResults,
  Map<Id,Id> mpFundAccountId_PendingAccountId){
    List<Pending_Request__c> lstPendingRequests = new
      List<Pending_Request__c>();
```

```
      for(Integer i=0 ; i<updateResults.size() ; i++){
        Pending_Request__c res = new Pending_Request__c(
          Record_Id__c = updateResults.get(i).getId(),
          Is_Processed__c = true, Status__c = 'Success' ) ;
      if (!updateResults.get(i).isSuccess()){
        res.Status__c = 'Error'; }

    //Get Id of record from Queue so that it can be updated

      if(mpFundAccountId_PendingAccountId.containsKey(res.Record_Id__c))
      {
        res.Id = mpFundAccountId_PendingAccountId.get(res.Record_Id__c);
      }

    //create list of result to be updated
      lstPendingRequests.add(res);
    }

    //Perform DML operation to update final status of records in Queue
    saveResultToPendingObject(lstPendingRequests);
  }
  /* * upsert results to "Pending Requests" object with
   * success or error status
   */
  private void saveResultToPendingObject(List<Pending_Request__c>
  lstPendingRequests){
    if(!lstPendingRequests.isEmpty()) {
      Database.upsert(lstPendingRequests, false );
    }
  }
}
```

The key element in this class is the usage of the `For Update` clause of SOQL. This clause can be used in SOQL to lock the records in advance so that other processes can not access the same records. Locking these records will be maintained by the program until the execution is completed.

The class performs the following operations:

1. It retrieves pending items from the queue (`Pending_Request__c`).
2. It identifies the amount to be added to the fund account (stored in `Parameter1__c`).
3. It locks and retrieves all the funding accounts that are to be updated.
4. It invokes an active object in a loop to perform operations.
5. It commits records updated by active objects.
6. It retrieves the result of the DML operation and updates all the records in the queue with a success or error status.

It's time to add a class that can be invoked from anywhere in an application to enqueue a request. The following class can be used for this purpose:

```
public class Enqueue_ActiveObject {
   /*
    * This method calls Active object pattern to update Account
    * which is Race condition proof
    */
   public static void addFund(String accountName, Decimal amount){
      List<Fund_Account__c> lstfundAcc = [SELECT Available_Fund__c FROM
Fund_Account__c WHERE NAME =: accountName LIMIT 1];
      //Enqueue request to be processed by Scheduler
        if(!lstfundAcc.isEmpty())
        {
         Pending_Request__c recordForQueue = new Pending_Request__c(
            Record_Id__c = lstfundAcc[0].id ,
            Parameter1__c = String.valueOf(amount),
            Operation_Type__c = 'Add_Amount');
         insert recordForQueue ;
        }
    }
}
```

This class contains the `addFund` public method that accepts two parameters: the account name and amount to be added.

Now, we need a scheduler that will check the queue and perform an operation on it:

```
public class Scheduler_ActiveObject implements Schedulable{

    public void execute(SchedulableContext ctx) {
        new AddFund_Service_ActiveObject().execute();
    }
}
```

As we can see the `Scheduler` class is very simple, and we are simply invoking the service class.

We cannot have the `Scheduler` class running continuously in Salesforce, and also, the minimum time interval for the scheduler is 1 hour. This means that the pending request records can only be processed at 60 minute intervals. Alternatively, we can schedule the Apex class to execute with a difference of 10 minutes, by starting six jobs for the same `Scheduler` class.

The following anonymous code can be executed to start six jobs for the `Scheduler_ActiveObject` class. We need to use the `System.schedule` method to schedule these jobs:

```
Scheduler_ActiveObject m = new Scheduler_ActiveObject();
String sch = '0 0 0/1 1/1 * ? * ';
String jobID = system.schedule('Active Object Scheduler', sch, m);
Scheduler_ActiveObject m1 = new Scheduler_ActiveObject();
String sch1 = '0 10 0/1 1/1 * ? * ';
String jobID1 = system.schedule('Active Object Scheduler - 10 Min',
sch1, m1);
Scheduler_ActiveObject m2 = new Scheduler_ActiveObject();
String sch2 = '0 20 0/1 1/1 * ? * ';
String jobID2 = system.schedule('Active Object Scheduler - 20 Min',
sch2, m2);
Scheduler_ActiveObject m3 = new Scheduler_ActiveObject();
String sch3 = '0 30 0/1 1/1 * ? * ';
String jobID3 = system.schedule('Active Object Scheduler - 30 Min',
sch3, m3);
Scheduler_ActiveObject m4 = new Scheduler_ActiveObject();
String sch4 = '0 40 0/1 1/1 * ? * ';
String jobID4 = system.schedule('Active Object Scheduler - 40 Min',
sch4, m4);
Scheduler_ActiveObject m5 = new Scheduler_ActiveObject();
String sch5 = '0 50 0/1 1/1 * ? * ';
String jobID5 = system.schedule('Active Object Scheduler - 50 Min',
sch5, m5);
```

The preceding technique will help us process a queue every ten minutes.

The following diagram shows how different layers are working in the active object pattern and are decoupled from each other. The `invocation` method (the service class) is decoupled from its execution (an active object).

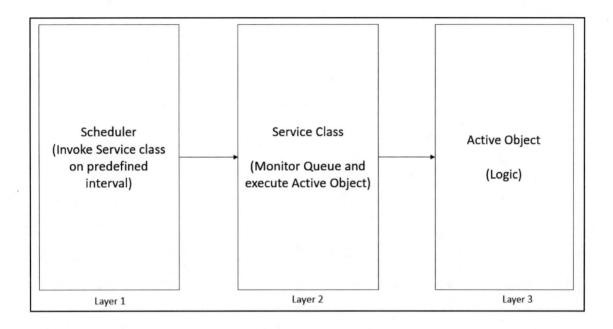

The following figure shows the class diagram of the active object pattern that we implemented in this example:

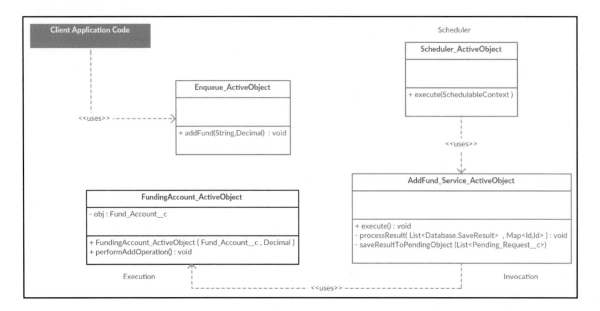

As discussed earlier in this chapter, we saw that the standard Salesforce user interface is concurrency safe when two different users try to update the same record. Internally, it does not seem to be using the `For Update` SOQL clause, as in that case, other users would not even be able to open the edit page. What we think, however, is not mentioned in any white paper or documentation, is that, internally Salesforce checks SystemModstamp of a record, and if it doesn't match and if someone has already modified the record after opening the edit page, it throws an error saying that the record is modified by someone else.

Points to consider

It is recommended that you use the active object pattern wherever a shared resource is accessed very frequently.

Summary

In this chapter, we learnt that Apex is very different from other programming languages when it comes to handling concurrency issues. Due to these differences, we cannot use many concurrent design patterns that are accepted by the industry, in Apex. In the active object design pattern, we have used the `For Update` SOQL clause to achieve a lock on a record. The standard Salesforce user interface is concurrency safe for different users but not for the same user. However, Apex is not at all concurrency safe, and we need to take extra steps to avoid these issues.

The following are the key points of our example as discussed earlier:

- This design pattern mainly consists of a queue, scheduler, and an active class as key components.
- This pattern decouples the execution method from its invocation.
- As we cannot have a shared queue in Apex, we have used a custom object pending request in our example.
- As we cannot have a scheduler run 24/7, we can run a scheduler every 10 minutes to fetch pending request records.
- We have used the `For Update` SOQL clause to lock a record in advance.
- The trade-off of using `For Update` is that if the execution takes more than 10 seconds, then other waiting processes trying to get the same record will end up with the `Unable to lock record` error.

6

Anti-patterns and Best Practices

We have come a long way from understanding the common software development problems and their solutions. Indeed, there must be some scenarios wherein it feels like an overkill or overdesign and yet some solutions may seem better than the design patterns. The idea behind design patterns is to find a structured and robust solution for common problems and not for specific problems. As problems keep on evolving, so will the solutions.

With our development experience and knowledge of design patterns, we can identify the best solutions or design patterns for code development and structuring. Similarly, there are some development solutions, which are regarded as bad solutions or anti-patterns.

Numerous anti-patterns could be listed in a book, but we are trying to highlight some very common pitfalls or bad solutions from a Salesforce customization standpoint.

Over usage of formula fields

Often, Salesforce configuration options are suggested as the first option or solution to any given problem. For example, the formula field. Formula fields are fast and easy ways to show calculated field values driven from the same or related objects (parents or grandparents). Formulas are easy to create and manage and are very handy when values are to be shown dynamically.

However, we should understand how a formula field really works under the hood. Formula fields are calculated fields (values are not physically stored), which are calculated every time a record is retrieved. The formula field value gets calculated only if it is a part of the retrieval process. This means that an additional calculation is to be performed for each object record that is retrieved. Now, this will not impact when you are merely looking at the record in view mode or are retrieving a limited number of records. But when you retrieve bulk records via code or reports, the use of more and more formula fields degrades the system performance. Furthermore, when formula fields are used in queries or report conditions, this further degrades the application performance. The next two sections describe the two types of formula field.

The deterministic formula field

A formula field is said to be *deterministic* when the value of the formula field changes only when the related record or field gets changed. For example, if we want to have a formula field to show 20% of the amount field, then it can be written as follows:

```
Formula Field = 0.2 x Amount
```

The preceding formula will change only when the dependent amount field gets changed.

The nondeterministic formula field

A formula field is said to be *nondeterministic* when the value of the formula field changes without the related record or field being modified. For example, if we want to detect whether the logged-in user is the owner of the record or not, the following formula can be used:

```
Formula Field =  IF( OwnerId =  $User.Id , true, false )
```

In the preceding formula field, its value will vary as per the logged-in user even though there is no update on the record.

To improve the performance, we can contact the Salesforce support team to enable a custom index on the formula field. However, indexing can be done only on the deterministic formula field. You can read more about this approach on the official Salesforce developer blog at `https://devel oper.salesforce.com/blogs/engineering/2013/03/force-com-f ormula-fields-indexes-and-performance-gotchas.html`.

Functional decomposition

Usually, a developer starts building a trigger or page controller and ends up writing all the business logic within the trigger or controller itself. It is definitely easy and fast but hard to maintain.

Say, for example, we have to develop a Visualforce page with the custom functionality of generating an invoice. So, we begin our controller, as follows:

```
public class GenerateInvoiceController{
    public Invoice__c Invoice {get; set;}
    //generate invoice
    public void generateInvoice(){
        if(validate(Invoice )){
            insert Invoice ;
        }
        else{
            // handle validation errors
        }
    }
    //validate invoice
    public Boolean validate(Invoice__c Invoice){
        Boolean isValid = false;
        // validation logic
        return isValid;
    }
}
```

A key thing that is missing here is understanding that Apex is an OOP language. It is very important to understand that in an object-oriented paradigm, the benefit that we can derive from a system is **to think from object aspects** and accordingly decompose the functionality in one or more classes. So, in our preceding example, it would be advisable to create a separate InvoiceService class that can contain all the business logic related to the invoice generation, and it should be used by the GenerateInvoiceController class to achieve the business functionality:

```
public class InvoiceService{

    public static Invoice__c createInvoice(Invoice__c invoice){
        if(validate(invoice)){
            insert invoice;
        }
        return invoice;
    }
    //validate invoice
    public static Boolean validate(Invoice__c Invoice){
```

```
        Boolean isValid = false;
        // validation logic
        return isValid;
    }
}


public class GenerateInvoiceController{
    public Invoice__c Invoice {get; set;}
    //generate invoice
    public void generateInvoice(){
        InvoiceService.createInvoice(Invoice);
    }
}
```

This new code structure helps us make a more modular and reusable code base. Now, this service can be easily reused by a trigger or a web service where there is a requirement for the same business process.

As discussed in the previous chapters, the central idea in designing and implementing design patterns is segregating separate concerns in separate classes. Similarly, it is advisable to build various classes (service, helper, utility, and so on) to help maintain the business functionality in a much more scalable and reusable approach. This greatly helps in easy code maintenance and high code reusability.

Controller classes should only contain logic to interact with the view (the user interface) and invoke appropriate helper/service/utility classes to achieve the business functionality. Similarly, a trigger should also include only the conditional logic and should make use of the helper/service/utility classes to achieve business functionality. Web service classes should also follow the same principle.

Ignoring the equals() and hashcode() methods while performing object comparison

Consider the following Apex class:

```
global class DealInfo {
    public Integer amount {get;set;}
    public String amountCurrency {get;set;}
}
```

Now, we are in a situation where we need to sort a list of objects from the preceding class. Let's run the following anonymous code:

```
DealInfo o = new DealInfo();
o.amount = 200;
o.amountCurrency = 'USD';

DealInfo o1 = new DealInfo();
o1.amount = 100;
o1.amountCurrency = 'USD';
List<DealInfo> lstDeals = new List<DealInfo>{o,o1};
lstDeals.sort();
```

If you are expecting the list to get sorted, then it's not so. We get the following error from Apex:

```
System.ListException: One or more of the items in this list is not
Comparable.
```

Salesforce already supports sorting primitive datatypes. However, to support the sorting capabilities for objects, such as wrapper classes or lists, we need to implement the `Comparable` interface provided by Apex. The `Comparable` interface forces the class to implement the following method:

```
global Integer compareTo(Object compareTo) {
    // Your comparison logic here
}
```

The `compareTo` method returns the integer value using the following rules:

- 0 means that both the records are the same
- >0 means that the current record is greater than the record to be compared
- <0 means that the current record is smaller than the record to be compared

As per the best practices, the value should be returned only when two objects are exactly **equal**.

So, a developer came up with the following code:

```
global class DealInfo implements Comparable  {
    public Integer amount {get;set;}
    public String amountCurrency {get;set;}
    //Implement "compareTo" method from Comparable interface
    global Integer compareTo(Object objToCompare) {
        DealInfo obj = (DealInfo) objToCompare ;
        //compare two objects
        if(this == obj){
            return 0;
        }
        return this.amount - obj.amount;
    }
}
```

The preceding code is not correct because to compare two objects, the == operator is used in the code snippet. This operator only compares the reference (address) of the objects and does not consider their actual content. So, we should use the equals method to compare objects in Apex.

After this discussion, an implementation of the compareTo method should look something like the following code snippet:

```
global class DealInfo implements Comparable  {
    public integer amount {get;set;}
    public String amountCurrency {get;set;}
    //Implement "compareTo" method from Comparable interface
    global Integer compareTo(Object objToCompare) {
        DealInfo obj = (DealInfo) objToCompare ;

        //Check if both objects are equal
        if(this.equals(obj)){
            return 0;
        }

        //Which object is greater than other
        return this.amount - obj.amount;
    }
}
```

There may be many developers out there who knowingly or unknowingly ignore the importance of the `equals()` and `hashcode()` methods while implementing the `Comparable` interface.

In the preceding code, we should use the `equals()` method. The preceding code is not yet correct.

To understand the problem in detail, execute the following anonymous code:

```
DealInfo o = new DealInfo();
o.amount = 200;
o.amountCurrency = 'USD';

DealInfo o1 = new DealInfo();
o1.amount = 200;
o1.amountCurrency = 'USD';

System.assertEquals(o, o1);
```

In the preceding code, when we try to check whether both the objects are equal using the `System.assertEquals()` method, we will receive an error saying that the objects are not the same as expected:

```
Line: 9, Column: 1 System.AssertException: Assertion Failed: Expected:
DealInfo:[amount=200, amountCurrency=USD], Actual: DealInfo:[amount=200,
amountCurrency=USD]
```

Both the records are exactly the same but why does the assertion still fail? This is because Apex doesn't know how to compare the two objects, and it's the developer's job to implement the equals method to instruct Salesforce to determine equality between two objects. Along with `equals()`, we should implement the `hashcode()` method as well. Hashcodes are used by the platform to index the object location in heap memory. Another reason why we should implement `hashcode()` is that Salesforce supports Apex classes as keys in maps and sets. If we do not implement `hashcode()`, then the same object would not be retrieved if it's used as a key in a map or a set.

As a best practice, the following guidelines should be followed while overriding the equals() method:

1. Check whether the record to be compared has the same location in memory. For this, we can use the *exact equality operator* (= = =) available in Apex.
2. Check whether a record to be compared is null.
3. Check whether both the records are of the same type to avoid typecasting an error.
4. Use the actual logic to see whether the content of the two objects is the same or not.

 All the available operators in Apex are listed in the official documentation page at `https://developer.salesforce.com/docs/atlas.en-us.apexcode.meta/apexcode/langCon_apex_expressions_operators_understanding.htm`.

General contracts between the and `equals()` hashcode() and equals() method in Apex are as follows:

- If two objects are equal, then their hashcode must also be the same
- If the hashcode is invoked multiple times on the same object in the same transaction, then the value should not be changed if none of the fields have been modified

Considering all the points that we discussed, the following code snippet is the correct implementation of the `equals()`, `hashcode()`, and `compareTo()` methods:

```
global class DealInfo implements Comparable {
    public Integer amount {get;set;}
    public String amountCurrency {get;set;}
    //Implement "compareTo" method from Comparable interface
    global Integer compareTo(Object objToCompare) {
        DealInfo obj = (DealInfo) objToCompare ;
        if(this.equals(obj)){
            return 0;
        }
        return this.amount - obj.amount;
    }
    //Override equals() method
    public Boolean equals(Object o) {
        //Rule 1
        if (this === o) {
            return true;
        }
```

```
        //Rule 2
        if ( (o == null) || !(o instanceof DealInfo) ) {
            return false;
        }
        //Rule 3
        DealInfo obj = (DealInfo)o;
        if(obj.amount == this.amount && obj.amountCurrency ==
this.amountCurrency)
        {
            return true;
        }
        return false;
    }
    //Override hashcode() method
    public Integer hashCode() {
        return this.amount  + this.amountCurrency.hashcode();
    }

}
```

Circular dependencies

There are multiple situations where the developer accidentally creates a circular
dependency between Apex classes, triggers, or even in object relationships. There are a few
programming languages that detect circular dependency between classes during
compilation. Unfortunately, Apex can only generate errors at runtime.

Circular dependency in Apex classes

We will understand circular dependency using the following two Apex classes:

```
public class ClassA {
    public ClassA(){
        ClassB b = new ClassB();
        System.debug('*** Class A Constructor ');
    }

}

public class ClassB {
    public ClassB()
    {
        ClassA a = new ClassA();
        System.debug('*** Class B Constructor ');
```

```
    }
  }
```

As we can see in the preceding code, a constructor of Class A calls a constructor of Class B, resulting in a error if we try to instantiate any class.

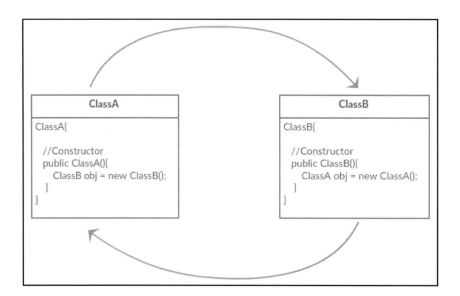

Run the following anonymous code:

```
ClassA a = new ClassA();
```

After executing the preceding code, we get the following error:

System.LimitException: Maximum stack depth reached: 1001

A code structure like this, where the two methods directly or indirectly depend on each other is known as the *circular dependency* anti-pattern.

Circular dependency in triggers

A developer can create circular dependency accidentally in triggers as well. Assume that the following trigger is written in Account for the before update event:

```
trigger Account_CD on Account (before update) {
```

```
    Set<Id> setAccId = Trigger.newMap.keyset();
    //Get all child contacts of Account
    List<Contact> lstContact = [SELECT NAME FROM Contact WHERE AccountId IN
:setAccId];
    for(Contact c : lstContact){
        c.Description = 'Updated from Account Trigger';
    }
    if(!lstContact.isEmpty())
    {
        update lstContact;
    }
}
```

In the preceding trigger, whenever any Account record is updated, we need to update the Description field in the related child Contacts.

Now assume that the following trigger is written in the Contact object for the before update event:

```
trigger Contact_CD on Contact (before update) {

    Set<Id> setAcc = new Set<Id>();
    //Get Account Id from Contact
    for(Contact c : Trigger.New)
    {
        if(c.AccountId != null)
        {
            setAcc.add(c.AccountId);
        }
    }
    //Get all parent Accounts and update their description field
    List<Account> lstAcc = [SELECT Name FROM Account Where Id IN :setAcc];
    for(Account acc : lstAcc)
    {
        acc.Description = 'updated from Contact Trigger';
    }
    if(!lstAcc.isEmpty())
    {
        update lstAcc;
    }
}
```

The preceding trigger will show that whenever the Contact is updated on the record, the related parent account's description field will also be updated.

It's time to test these triggers. First, create a sample `Account` record and then create a child contact record. When we try to update a child contact, a trigger will be created, and you need to update the parent account record, and the trigger written in the parent account record will again update the child contact record, and thus it will cause a recursion error, as shown in the following screenshot:

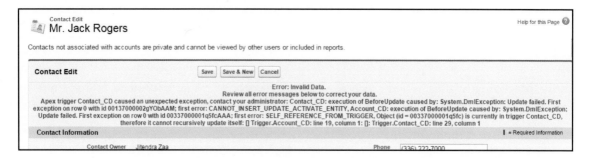

We have to be very careful while writing any trigger and this scenario needs to be considered, as this can be caught only at runtime while the end users are using the system.

Circular dependency is detected by Salesforce objects as well out of the box. The `Account` object has the standard parent account field. If we try to create a self-relationship by selecting the same account record in the parent account field, then Salesforce generates an error of circular dependency, as shown in the following figure:

Other examples

- A controller calls the service class method and the service class method, in turn, uses the controller's static constant
- A controller calls the service class method, the service class method calls the utility class method, and the utility class method further calls the controller/service class method, as shown in the following diagram (**Fig a**):

In both the preceding examples, we will not get any error. However, we may face issues while deploying classes in the layered approach. The layered approach means deploying the utility classes first followed by the service and controller classes.

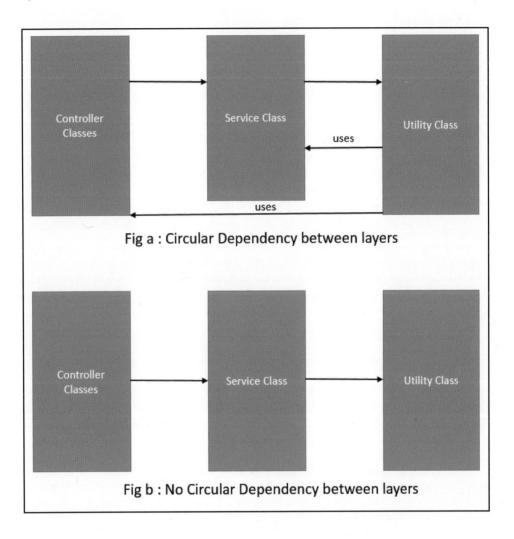

Fig a : Circular Dependency between layers

Fig b : No Circular Dependency between layers

The ignoring toString() method

Consider the following Apex class:

```
public class ToStringDemo {
    public String companyName {get;set;}
    public String city {get;set;}
}
```

A developer can print any important information about this class by running the following anonymous Apex code:

```
ToStringDemo obj = new ToStringDemo();
obj.companyName = 'Salesforce';
obj.city = 'SFO';
System.debug(obj);
```

The output is as follows:

```
ToStringDemo:[city=SFO, companyName=Salesforce]
```

In the preceding code, we are trying to print an object for debugging purposes. Internally, Apex calls the `toString()` method. As we have not overridden it, Salesforce uses its predefined `className:[variable1=value, variable2=value, ...]` format to print the object value:

Ignoring the override of the `toString()` method is considered as an anti-pattern and we should implement it whenever possible.

 Every class in Apex is by default a child of the `Object` class. So, all the classes inherit methods provided by the `Object` class. For example, `equals()`, `hashcode()`, and `toString()` are a few methods from the `Object` class, which are by default inherited by all the classes in Apex.

It is possible to change the preceding output format. We will override the `toString()` method in our Apex class, as shown in the following code:

```
public class ToStringDemo {
    public String companyName {get;set;}
    public String city {get;set;}
    //override toString()
    public override String toString(){
        return companyName+' is situated at '+city;
    }
}
```

If we rerun the same anonymous code, then the output will be as follows:

```
Salesforce is situated at SFO
```

Now, this output is more meaningful as compared to the standard `toString()` method.

Avoid the God class

This is one of the very common issues in application development, where a class either has too many lines of code or knows too much about the application or plays too many roles in an application. This type of a class is known as the *God class*. For example, it is a best practice that triggers should not contain business logic, and therefore we create helper classes. Sometimes, we create utility classes as well. By the time the development phase of a project progresses, these classes become huge and are referred to by many other classes. In such situations, refactoring of code becomes very tough and may break other parts of the application. As expected, developers avoid changing anything that exists in the God class, and therefore these types of classes contain many lines of code, which may not be used anywhere.

 If this class is used indirectly by any Apex scheduled jobs, then it is serialized, and further updating the class is restricted by the platform while a job is in progress.

As per the best practices and the single responsibility principle, we should avoid these types of classes in our application.

Error hiding

Exception/error handling is a very common process. In fact, it is one of the most prominent topics when learning a new programming language. Exception handling helps programmers to manage adverse conditions and ensures that the software/application can recover from any expected or unexpected failures. Often, programmers ignore the importance of exception handling, which results in:

- Erroneous screens/messages being visible to end users
- Catastrophic program failures leaving programs/data in an unstable state
- Incorrect/improper error messages being displayed to users

The first step in exception handling is to ensure that all the probable areas should be equipped with an appropriate exception handling logic. As commonly stated "at minimum, all publicly accessible methods should have an appropriate try/catch". It solves the first point mentioned earlier, that is, erroneous screens/messages being visible to end users.

Let's focus on the second and third points now.

In Apex, database transactions are automatically committed; that is, any database transaction will be committed only if there are no unhandled exceptions.

Similar to various other programming languages, Apex has a top-level exception class as well that can handle any type of exception (excluding exceptions related to governor limits).

Now, let's take a look at a very simple example. Let's take a controller method, which saves an account:

```
public class GenerateAccountController {
    Account NewAccount {get; set;}
    //..some awesome variable to be used by class

    public GenerateAccountController(){
        NewAccount = new Account();
    }
    //..some awesome code here

    public void createAccount(){
        insert NewAccount;
    }
}
```

In the preceding example, it is quite evident that any exception thrown while inserting an account will result in a non-user-friendly error message being displayed to the user, as shown in the following figure:

As per the first point discussed earlier, we should avoid erroneous screens for end users. So, let's wrap the code in the try-catch block, as shown in the following code:

```
public class GenerateAccountController {
    public Account NewAccount {get; set;}
    public GenerateAccountController(){
        NewAccount = new Account();
    }
    public void createAccount(){
        try{
          insert NewAccount;
        }
        catch(Exception ex){
        }
    }
}
```

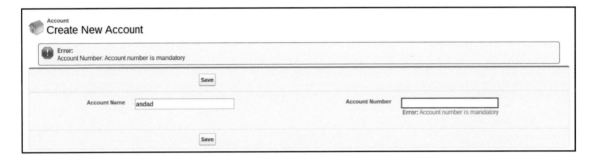

This is a fantastic example of Visualforce's clever error handling and notification process, even though the catch block is empty in code. Here, any validation rule that is attached to a field will result in an error being displayed at the top as well as at the field level automatically (if `apex:inputField` is used).

If we use `apex:inputText` instead of `apex:inputField`, the error with the associated field will still be displayed at the top of the page but not at the field level.
To display error messages attached to the page, use the `apex:pageMessages` component.

It is a good start, but it only handles validation errors appropriately. Let's modify our code even further and try to create a contact as soon as an account is created:

```
public class GenerateAccountController {
    public Account NewAccount {get; set;}
    public GenerateAccountController(){
        NewAccount = new Account();
    }
    public void createAccount(){
        try{
         insert NewAccount;
            Contact c;
            //intentionally contact c is not initialized
            insert c;
        }
        catch(Exception ex){
        }
    }
}
```

In the preceding code, we will get an error while inserting the contact because we did not initialize the contact object. When the preceding controller is executed, we will notice that:

- The account is inserted successfully because the exception in our transaction was handled and there were no unhandled exceptions. The data was partially committed because the account was saved without the contact.
- No error message is displayed to the user because our catch block doesn't display any error message to the user.

This is a classic example of *error hiding*. We are hiding the errors and not handling them. This anti-pattern signifies improper exception handling processes. Sometimes, error hiding can be unavoidable. For example, in the case of unexpected errors or web service integrations, where there can be myriads of errors and there is no need to handle them separately. In cases where we need to hide an error, we can either show a generic message to end users or log it. But, as a good practice, any known or expected error should be handled appropriately to ensure system stability and user-friendliness.

As we can see in the preceding code snippet, this is the behavior that we definitely do not want. Either accounts and contacts should be saved together or nothing should be saved. So, we modify our code to instruct the Force.com platform to not commit any data unless the entire operation is completed successfully:

```
public class GenerateAccountController {
    public Account NewAccount {get; set;}
    public GenerateAccountController(){
```

```
            NewAccount = new Account();
    }
    public void createAccount(){
        System.savepoint sp = Database.setSavepoint();
        try{
         insert NewAccount;
            Contact c;
            insert c;
        }
        catch(Exception ex){
            Database.rollback(sp);
        }
    }
}
```

We have to consider the following limitations while using transactions in Apex:

1. In the case of multiple save points, when we roll back to a save point, all the save points created after this save point will become invalid. Trying to roll back to those save points will cause a runtime error.

2. Each rollback counts against the DML operation.

3. If an object is inserted and then rolled back, it will not clear the ID from the object in memory. If you try to reinsert the same object, it will cause a runtime error.

This additional code helps ensure that the entire operation, that is, the insertion of the account and contact, are treated as one transaction. In case of a failure, the entire transaction is rolled back. Only when the entire transaction is successfully executed, Apex auto-commits the entire transaction. Now, when we run this code, we will see that the page refreshes but no account is created. However, we are still not displaying any error message. In the following code, we added the logic to display the error message in the catch block:

```
public class GenerateAccountController {
    public Account NewAccount {get; set;}
    public String ContactLimit {get; set;}
    public GenerateAccountController(){
        NewAccount = new Account();
    }
    public void createAccount(){
        System.savepoint sp = Database.setSavepoint();
        try{
         //insert NewAccount;
            if(Newaccount.Type == 'Prospect'){
                Contact c = new Contact(LastName = NewAccount.Name,
```

```
                                          Phone = NewAccount.Phone,
                                          Limit__c =
Integer.valueOf(ContactLimit),
                                          Accountid = NewAccount.id);
                    insert c;
          }
        }
        catch(Exception ex){
            /* rollback transaction */
            Database.rollback(sp);
            /* display error message */
            ApexPages.Message msg = new
ApexPages.Message(ApexPages.Severity.ERROR, ex.getMessage());
            System.debug(ex);
            Apexpages.addMessage(msg);
        }
      }
    }
```

Now, after the execution, the user will see the following message on the page:

The preceding code fulfills all the three issues that we discussed at the start of this topic to demonstrate how to avoid the error hiding anti-pattern.

Hard-coding

Now, this is the most discussed, most noted, and most emphasized anti-pattern that exists. It is so common and widespread that ever since programming began this anti-pattern has existed and still prevails. As you probably already know that using any embedded values (string literals, numbers, Ids, and so on) within the code is termed hard-coding and is an anti-pattern.

As per general programming, hard-coding values is considered as a bad practice, and instead, any such values should be handled via the available configuration options. In Salesforce, we have custom labels, custom settings, custom metadata types, and caching or custom objects.

In Apex, Ids are another important set of values, which should never be hard-coded, as they can change across different Salesforce environments.

Some tips to avoid hard-coding are as follows:

- Retrieve Ids of standard objects (profile, record type, reports, e-mail template, and so on) by either using dynamic Apex or querying appropriate setup sObjects.
- Use custom labels, custom settings, and custom metadata appropriately to avoid hard-coding.

Even though a custom label is one of the options used to avoid hard-coding. However, while deploying a custom label, its data also gets deployed, which may cause an unexpected behavior.Custom settings or custom metadata are the preferred options to avoid hard-coding.

Magic strings and numbers

Using unnamed strings or numbers in a class is called *magic strings and numbers*.

The following code snippet explains this:

```
List<Opportunity> lstOpp = [SELECT Id, Name , StageName from Opportunity
Where StageName = 'Under Verification'] ;
//some awesome code
```

In the preceding code, we are trying to fetch all the opportunities in the Under Verfication stage. In this code snippet, a string literal is directly used to compare the stage without any variables or configurations. There may be many other classes as well where developers could have used the same approach. In this example, it's the string; however, the same applies to numbers as well. Now assume that our company wants to rename the stage from Under Verification to Pending Review. Imagine the amount of work that needs to be done to perform the impact analysis and incorporate the changes. If we had used a constant variable or configuration, this situation could have been avoided.

Inheritance hell

As we all understand the basic principles of OOPs, inheritance is one of the most used OOP principle. It is definitely very handy in the enterprise software design as it helps extend the existing functionalities and helps improve/enhance the system progressively.

But this benefit can become a bane when not handled properly. Normally, inheritance is used when we want to generalize a behavior/functionality and then extend it on an *as-needed basis*. In reality, sometimes the parent class becomes so bloated that all the child classes unnecessarily carry (or inherit) nonrelated attributes/functionalities. This is called **inheritance hell**.

Furthermore, because Apex doesn't allow multiple inheritance (using classes), inheritance hell further leads to more issues if a given child class needs to extend functionalities from two different classes.

To avoid inheritance hell, we can use the strategy pattern. It helps enhance the capabilities of a class by separating the functional logic from the main class.

SOQL inside a loop

Salesforce being a multi-tenant cloud platform, monitors each tenant's (organization's) process load, data usage, and so on to ensure that no tenant can cause an impact on the other tenants' processes. To achieve this, Salesforce imposes governor limits. Governor limits define the system usage allowance available to each tenant and ensures that any tenant crossing those limits is restricted to further impact the system. One such transaction level Apex limit is *total number of SOQL queries issued in a single request*. At present, the limit is 100 for synchronous transactions (Apex methods and triggers) and 200 for asynchronous transactions (batch Apex, future methods, and so on). So, if your code issues even one extra SOQL than the allowed limit within the code, then Salesforce will throw a governor limit exception.

For example, the following code is an Apex trigger built to automatically populate the value of an SLA field on a `Contact` record by taking its values from the account level SLA field:

```
trigger ContactCreation on Contact (before insert) {
    for(Contact newContact : Trigger.new){
        Account account = [select id, SLA__c from Account where id =
:newContact.Accountid];
        newContact.SLA__c = account.SLA__c;
    }
}
```

Now, this code fulfills the business requirement and correctly retrieves accounts and populates the contact's SLA field. But we notice that the SOQL query is placed within the `for` loop. So, for each `Contact` record inserted, the code will perform a query.

However, when more than 100 records are inserted together, this trigger will fail. It will fail because the number of SOQL queries exceeded the limit (the SOQL limit exception).

In order to bulkify our code, we will refactor the code to ensure that only one query is executed within the trigger, irrespective of the record count, with the help of collections in Apex:

```
trigger ContactCreation on Contact (before insert) {
    /* Iterate over all contacts to retrieve unique account ids */
    Set<Id> setAccountIds = new Set<id>();
    for(Contact newContact : Trigger.new){
        setAccountIds.add(newContact.AccountId);
    }
    /* Retrieve all related accounts and create a map of accounts */
    Map<id, Account> mapAccounts = new Map<id, Account>([select id, SLA__c
from Account where id in :setAccountIds]);
    /* Iterate over all contacts and populate SLA field */
    for(Contact newContact :Trigger.new){
        Account relatedAccount = mapAccounts.get(newContact.AccountId);
        newContact.SLA__c = relatedAccount.SLA__c;
    }
}
```

You can also use SOQL `for` loops to efficiently handle large datasets within your Apex code. It provides a smart auto-chunking mechanism wherein the records are retrieved and processed in chunks, hence avoiding the maximum heap size governor limit (the current limit for the maximum heap size is 6 MB for synchronous transactions and 12 MB for asynchronous transactions).

DML inside a loop

As in the case of the previous anti-pattern, Salesforce imposes another governor limit known as *total number of DML statements issued in a single request*. As the name implies, it restricts the number of **Data Manipulation Language (DML)** statements. For example, `insert`, `update`, `delete`, `undelete`, and so on.

 You can get a comprehensive list of all the DML statements in the official documentation at `https://developer.salesforce.com/docs/atlas .en-us.apexcode.meta/apexcode/apex_gov_limits.htm`.

Our business requirement is to create a contact for each account inserted. So, we developed our code, as follows:

```
trigger AccountCreation on Account (after insert) {
    /* Iterate over all accounts inserted */
    for(Account account : Trigger.new){
        /* generate new account */
        Contact c = new Contact(LastName = account.Name, accountid =
account.id);
        insert c;
    }
}
```

The preceding trigger will fail after processing more than 150 records, as the Apex governor limit on the number of DML statements within an Apex transaction is 150. In order to handle larger datasets, we can club all the records qualifying for DML together in a collection and invoke a single DML operation, as follows:

```
trigger AccountCreation on Account (after insert) {
    List<Contact> lstNewContacts = new List<Contact>();
    /* Iterate over all accounts inserted */
    for(Account account : Trigger.new){
        /* generate new account */
        Contact c = new Contact(LastName = account.Name, accountid =
account.id);
        lstNewContacts.add(c);
    }
    /* insert all new contacts */
    insert lstNewContacts;
}
```

Downloading the example code
You can download the example code files for this book from your account at http://www.packtpub.com. If you purchased this book elsewhere, you can visit http://www.packtpub.com/support and register to have the files e-mailed directly to you. You can download the code files by following these steps:

- Log in or register to our website using your e-mail address and password.
- Hover the mouse pointer on the SUPPORT tab at the top.
- Click on Code Downloads & Errata.
- Enter the name of the book in the Search box.
- Select the book for which you're looking to download the code files.
- Choose from the drop-down menu where you purchased this book from.
- Click on Code Download.

You can also download the code files by clicking on the Code Files button on the book's webpage at the Packt Publishing website. This page can be accessed by entering the book's name in the Search box. Please note that you need to be logged in to your Packt account.
Once the file is downloaded, please make sure that you unzip or extract the folder using the latest version of:

- WinRAR / 7-Zip for Windows
- Zipeg / iZip / UnRarX for Mac
- 7-Zip / PeaZip for Linux

Now, this code will run absolutely fine, even for larger datasets. In the preceding code, we issue only one DML statement instead of issuing one DML statement for each record. So, whether the trigger is being executed for one record or one hundred records, it will always execute only one DML statement. Hence, the trigger is now *bulkified* and can handle bulk data effectively.

Summary

In this chapter, we discussed and listed some of the most common mistakes made by developers. These mistakes are also termed as anti-patterns. Some develop invalid code that can only be detected at runtime, hard-coding, and so on. The purpose of writing this chapter is to let you know about the potential issues so that you keep them in mind while developing any code in Apex.

Developing code is an art. Every developer is an artist and follows some unique styles. This book will suggest some of industry-wide accepted patterns to solve repeated problems faced in the Salesforce application development. However, developers can improvise while implementing these design patterns.

Design patterns may or may not provide exact solutions to our coding problems; however, they guide you to design better code architecture and can help you ideate new solutions.

The motive of the design pattern is to design an application with loosely coupled layers and easy-to-maintain and reusable code. While developing the code, keep it in mind that *it is going to change in future*. How less and easily the code can be changed defines the proper usage of design principles and patterns.

Index